Ninja Foodi Grill cookbook 1000

1000 Affordable Savory Recipes for Ninja Foodi Smart XL Grill and Ninja Foodi AG301 Grill to Air Fry Roast Bake Dehydrate Broil and More

By Jessie Hill

Table of Contents

Description

Hunt down the sear, the sizzle, and the Air Fry crisp with the Ninja Foodi Grill and tasty recipe combination!

The scent of **char-grilled perfection** with the all-American outdoor cookout atmosphere, from the comfort of your kitchen, is now in your reach.

You are about to uncover a **mind-blowing** indoor grilling appliance to create all your **favorite grilled delicacies.**

The Ninja Foodi Grill cookbook for beginners is the perfect ammunition you need for your grilling expedition regardless of season and weather. It contains information on the following:

➢   Introduction to the Ninja Foodi Grill?

➢   The difference between the Ninja Foodi AG301 Grill and the Ninja Foodi Smart XL Grill.

➢   The Advantages of the Ninja Foodi Grill.

➢   The Usage, Cleaning, and Maintenance Tips.

➢   Frequently Asked Questions about the Grill.

➢   150 sizzling recipes to rival the best of them.

Enjoy!

Introduction

The Ninja Foodi brand has been dazzling us for years with insightful, convenient, and luxurious cooking appliances to transform our cooking game. And now, with the Ninja Foodi Grill, they have created an innovative way to recreate the impact of the BTU outdoor cooking power indoors with the taste and flavor of the food intact.

The superheated Cyclonic air, the high-density grill grate (ceramic coated), the multi-functional signature, and many other wonderful features are duplicated in the various models of the Ninja Foodi Grill series. The Smart XL Grill and the AG301 are solid examples. It is safe to declare success. Do you agree? This cookbook is here to help you begin the ultimate grilling adventure that promises to make you proud of what you cook anytime, anywhere.

Cook in style!

Chapter 1: Ninja Foodi Grill 101

What is the Ninja Foodi Grill?

The Ninja Foodi Grill is a multi-functional electricity-powered, countertop indoor cooking appliance. Due to their stainless steel design, Ninja Foodi grills are lighter to lift than other Grills.

Illustratively, both the Smart XL and the AG301 models produce 1760 watts of power to cook frozen foods to char-grilled wonders in 25 minutes. The Air crisp function helps to make guilt-free foods thanks to the minimal oil requirement. Brushing the food with oil before grilling reduces the fat/calorie content by 75%, producing healthy foods perfect for your diet requirements.

Comparatively, the Smart XL Grill is bigger than the AG301 grill. Therefore, it can cook up large quantities of food at once. The Ninja Foodi grills come in different sizes and dimensions, but they all deliver seared, sizzled, Crisp, char-flavored deliciousness.

Ninja Foodi Smart XL Grill VS Ninja Foodi AG301 Grill

For a broader appreciation of the miracle that is the Ninja Foodi Grill, it is imminent we examine these two contenders and their differences. This way, it becomes a no brainer to pick what fits your needs.

Characteristics	Ninja Foodi AG301 Grill	Ninja Foodi Smart XL Grill
Cooking programs	There are **5 cook programs**. Grill, Air crisp, Bake, Roast, and Dehydrate.	There are **6 cook programs**. Broil, Dehydrate, Air crisp, Roast, Bake, and Grill.
Smart temperature probe	Absent. You have to rely a bit on **guesswork** to attain that perfect doneness.	Dual sensor Present. To continuously monitor the temperature accuracy for even more perfect doneness. **Multi-task away**, since it cancels the need to watch over the food.
Smart cook system	Absent. Requires frequent checks and guesswork for satisfactory results.	Present. With 4 smart protein settings and 9 customizable doneness levels, all the work is done once you input the required setting. Just wait for your food to cook.

		You could be busy doing your laundry while you cook.
Weight	20 pounds	27.5 pounds
Dimension (L×W×H) inches	12.5 ×16.88×10.59 inches.	18.8 x 17.7 x 14 inches. Therefore, it is evident that this is the **larger option** for large-sized family dishes and 50% more grilling space.

Picture of Ninja Foodi AG301 Grill

Picture of Ninja Foodi Smart XL Grill

Components of Ninja Foodi Grill

The two contenders here have similar components with one or two exceptions. Size is also a dissimilar factor between the two.

Common components

- Ceramic-coated Grill grate
- Ceramic-coated Crisper basket
- Ceramic-coated Cooking pot
- Hood with convection fan to circulate hot air around the food.
- Removable splatter shield to prevent smoke and to protect the heating element from food splatters.
- Digital Control panel contains an LED screen to display temperature, time, and cooking function, and buttons to initiate them
- Cleaning brush and scraper to clean the grill grate and other accessories of baked-on grease and food residue.
- Air inlet and outlet vents
- Additional Accessories that do not come with all models include a griddle plate, veggie tray, kebab skewers, roasting rack,

Components unique to Foodi Smart XL Grill

- Food smart thermometer.
- Onboard thermometer storage attached to the side of the main unit.

Components unique to Foodi AG301 grill

The components of the Foodi AG301 grill are synonymous with the common components listed above. However, the appliance is smaller than the Smart XL Grill.

Advantages of using Ninja Foodi Grill

What are those features that set apart the Ninja Foodi grill above all other indoor grills?

- **Does not merely grill**: unlike other grill brands, the Ninja Foodi Grill brands can perform five to ten more functions; make barbecue, roast vegies, bake pastries, broil meats, and so on- all in one appliance!
- **Cyclonic grilling technology:** this one of a kind technology gives speed as well as utmost efficiency. The cyclonic air moves rapidly to surround all sides of your food for a caramelized char outer finish and a juicy evenly cooked inside in record time.
- **Frozen to sizzling hot char greatness:** there is no need to wait for your frozen meats, fish, and fries to defrost before you cook them. Set the time and temperature according to the recipe recommendation and get a char flavored meal in just a few minutes.

- **Flipping is not mandatory:** this feature gives perfect char marks on either side of your steak without flipping it, thanks to the surround-superheated cyclonic air that touches all sides of the food at once.
- **Technology to control grill intensity levels;** select low (400°), medium (450°), high (500°), and Max (510°) temperature level to get the doneness level (rare, medium-rare, medium, medium well, well) you want.
- **Easy to use:** the digital control panel makes selecting the cooking function effortless

Chapter 2: Tips for Usage, Cleaning, and Maintenance

1. Clean the unit after every use.
2. You may wash all accessories except the smart thermometer in a dishwasher. Only hand wash the thermometer with warm soapy water and a non-abrasive cloth/sponge. Rinse with clean water and then air dry or towel dry. Never dip the main unit in any fluid.
3. Soak accessories with tough grease stains in soapy water overnight to soften them. Rinse and dry thoroughly before use.
4. You are free to check your food while cooking. Since the timer freezes, the interruption does not affect the cooking process once you open the hood.
5. Study the the charts, instructions, cautions, and tables in the user guide for optimal use of the Foodi Grill.
6. Remember to preheat
7. When the cooking function stops, allow your food to rest for about 10 minutes inside the grill to allow the natural juices to redistribute throughout the protein.
8. Get a pair of oven mitts, a basting brush, a spatula, skewers, and tongs. They are necessary.

Chapter 3: Common FAQs for Ninja Foodi Grill

1. **What should I do to apply my favorite recipes to the Ninja Foodi Grill?** Select the bake setting, cut the recipe's temperature by 25°F, and check the food often to prevent overcooked results.

2. **Why did the unit trip the circuit breaker?** It tripped because you plugged your 1760 watts unit into a circuit breaker less than 15 amp.

3. **How can I skip preheating?** The grill function does not allow skipping preheating. However, press the preheat indicator again after pressing the start button to skip preheating for other functions

Chapter 4: Breakfast and Brunch

Tasty Ninja Baked Eggs

Tasty Ninja Baked Eggs is a great meal to have for breakfast or brunch-easy to prepare and provides your body with necessary nutrients.

Preparation time: 10 minutes
Cooking time: 20 minutes
Serves: 4

Ingredients To Use:

- 4 large eggs
- 1 pound of torn baby spinach, sauteed
- 7 ounces of chopped ham
- 4 Tbsp milk
- 1 Tbsp olive oil
- Cooking spray
- Salt and pepper, as desired

Step-by-Step Directions to Cook It:

1. Place the cooking pot into the Ninja Foodi Grill and ensure the splatter shield is in position. Close the hood.
2. Press the Bake button. Use the default temperature of 350°F and set the time for 20 minutes.
3. Press the start/stop button to preheat the appliance for 3 minutes.
4. Coat 4 ramekins with the cooking spray, and divide the sauteed baby spinach and ham into the ramekins.
5. Crack an egg into each ramekin.
6. Add equal amounts of milk. Add salt and pepper as desired
7. Arrange the ramekins into the preheated Ninja Foodi Grill and close the hood.

8. Serve Ninja-baked eggs.

Serving suggestions: Serve with freshly squeezed orange juice

Preparation and Cooking Tips: Preheat the appliance for best taste

Nutritional value per serving: Calories: 321kcal, Fat: 6g, Carb: 15g, Proteins: 12g

Ninja Breakfast Soufflé

Ninja Breakfast Soufflé is a savory meal perfect for breakfast. It is fun to eat and provides your body with good nutrients.

Preparation time: 10 minutes
Cooking time: 8minutes
Serves: 4

Ingredients To Use:

- 4 eggs, beaten
- 4 Tbsp of heavy cream
- A pinch of crushed red chili pepper
- 2 Tbsp of chopped parsley
- 2 Tbsp of chopped chives
- Salt and black pepper, as desired

Step-by-Step Directions to Cook It:

1. Place the cooking pot into the Ninja Foodi Grill and ensure the splatter shield is in position. Close the hood.
2. Press the Bake button. Use the default temperature of 350°F and set the time for 8minutes.
3. Press the start/stop button to preheat the appliance for 3 minutes.

4. Mix the eggs, heavy cream, chili pepper, parsley, chives, salt, and pepper in a bowl.
5. Divide equally into 4 souffle dishes
6. Arrange the dishes on the cooking pot of the Ninja Foodi Grill and close the hood.
7. Serve.

Serving suggestions: Serve with freshly squeezed orange juice

Preparation and Cooking Tips: The appliance pauses when the hood is opened and resumes cooking once the hood is closed. Lverage this while cooking

Nutritional value per serving: Calories: 300kcal, Fat: 7g, Carb: 15g, Proteins: 6g

Ham Pie

Ham pie has an awesome taste and is very filling

Preparation time: 10 minutes
Cooking time: 25 minutes
Serves: 6

Ingredients To Use:
- 2 eggs, beaten
- 2 cups of grated cheddar cheese
- 1 tbsp of grated parmesan
- 16 ounces of crescent rolls dough
- 2 cups of cooked, chopped ham
- Salt and black pepper, as desired
- Cooking spray

Step-by-Step Directions to Cook It:
1. Place the cooking pot into the Ninja Foodi Grill and ensure the splatter shield is in position. Close the hood.
2. Press the Bake button. Set the temperature to 300°F and adjust the time to 25 minutes.
3. Press the start/stop button to preheat the appliance for 3 minutes.
4. Mix the cheddar cheese, salt, pepper, and parmesan in a bowl and whisk thoroughly.
5. Grease a baking pan and press half of the dough rolls to the bottom of the pan.
6. Transfer the baking pan to the Ninja Foodi Grill and spread the egg mix over the rolls. Top with the ham
7. Cut the rest of the rolls into strips and arrange over the ham.
8. Close the hood.

Serving suggestions: Slice the pie and serve immediately

Preparation and Cooking Tips: Ensure to grease the baking pan before adding the dough rolls.

Nutritional value per serving: Calories: 400kcal, Fat: 27g, Carb: 22g, Proteins: 16g

Ninja Air-Baked Sandwich

Ninja Air-Baked sandwich is great for breakfast; it is tasty and fun to eat.

Preparation time: 10 minutes
Cooking time: 6 minutes
Serves: 2

Ingredients To Use:
- 4 halved English muffins
- 2 bacon strips
- 2 medium eggs
- Salt and black pepper, as desired

Step-by-Step Directions to Cook It:
1. Place the cooking pot into the Ninja Foodi Grill and ensure the splatter shield is in position. Close the hood.
2. Press the Bake button. Set the temperature to 392°F and time to6 minutes.
3. Press the start/stop button to preheat the appliance for 3 minutes.
4. Crack the eggs into the cooking pot and top with the bacon strips. Close the hood.
5. Divide the air fried eggs into halves.
6. Arrange one of the egg halves between two halved English muffins—season with salt and pepper.
7. Serve

Serving suggestions: Serve with Pineapple Juice

Preparation and Cooking Tips: Disregard the salt for a healthier meal

Nutritional value per serving: Calories: 261kcal, Fat: 5g, Carb: 12g, Proteins: 4g

Asparagus Frittata

Asparagus Frittata is a delicious meal to have for breakfast. It is a great way to include vegetables in your meal. It is nutritious.

Preparation time: 10 minutes
Cooking time: 5 minutes
Serves: 2

Ingredients To Use:
- 4 eggs, beaten
- 10 steamed asparagus tips
- 2 tbsp of grated parmesan
- Salt and black pepper, as desired

- 4 tbsp of milk
- Cooking spray

Step-by-Step Directions to Cook It:
1. Place the cooking pot into the Ninja Foodi Grill and ensure the splatter shield is in position. Close the hood.
2. Press the Bake button. Set the temperature to 400°F and adjust the time to 5 minutes.
3. Press the start/stop button to preheat the appliance for 3 minutes.
4. Mix the eggs, parmesan, salt, pepper, and milk in a bowl.
5. Add the asparagus to the cooking pot and cover with the egg mix
6. Toss
7. Close the hood of the Ninja Foodi Grill

Serving suggestions: Serve immediately

Preparation and Cooking Tips: Grease the cooking pot with cooking spray before preheating

Nutritional value per serving: Calories: 312kcal, Fat: 5g, Carb: 14g, Proteins: 2g

Breakfast Potatoes

With the Ninja Foodi Grill, the potatoes have a crispy finish. Simply delicious and crunchy!

Preparation time: 10 minutes
Cooking time: 35 minutes
Serves: 4

Ingredients To Use:
- 2 Tbsp of olive oil
- 3 potatoes, quartered
- 1 yellow onion, sliced

- 1 red bell pepper, sliced
- Salt and pepper, as desired
- 1 tsp of garlic powder
- 1 tsp of sweet paprika
- 1 tsp of onion powder

Step-by-Step Directions to Cook It:
1. Place the cooking pot into the Ninja Foodi Grill, then the crisper basket.
2. Ensure the splatter shield is in position and close the hood.
3. Press the air crisp button. Set the temperature to 370°F and set the time for 30 minutes.
4. Press the start/stop button to preheat the appliance for 3 minutes.
5. Coat the crisper basket with olive oil, add the potatoes, onion, onion powder, bell pepper, paprika, garlic powder, salt, and pepper.
6. Toss until well combined
7. Close the hood of the Ninja Foodi Grill.
8. Divide potatoes into 4 equal servings.

Serving suggestions: Serve with Pineapple Juice

Preparation and Cooking Tips: Always preheat for best flavor

Nutritional value per serving: Calories: 214kcal, Fat: 6g, Carb: 15g, Proteins: 4g

French Blackberry Toast

French blackberry toast is a delightful meal that leaves your taste buds excited.

Preparation time: 10 minutes
Cooking time: 20 minutes
Serves: 6

Ingredients To Use:
- 1 cup of warm blackberry jam
- 8 ounces of cubed cream cheese
- 4 eggs
- 12 ounces of cubed bread loaf
- 1 tsp vanilla extract
- 1 tsp cinnamon powder
- 2 cups of half and half
- Cooking spray
- ½ cup brown sugar

Step-by-Step Directions to Cook It:
1. Place the cooking pot into the Ninja Foodi Grill and ensure the splatter shield is in position. Close the hood.
2. Press the Bake button. Set the temperature to 300°F and adjust the time to 20 minutes.
3. Press the start/stop button to preheat the appliance for 3 minutes.
4. Add the blueberry jam to the cooking pot.
5. Layer with half of the bread cubes
6. Add the cream cheese
7. Top with the rest of the bread cubes and close the hood

Serving suggestions: Serve immediately

Preparation and Cooking Tips: Grease the cooking pot before preheating

Nutritional value per serving: Calories: 215kcal, Fat: 6g, Carb: 16g, Proteins: 6g

Cinnamon Toast

Cinnamon toast is easy to prepare, and with the Ninja Foodi Grill, the toast is extra crispy.

Preparation time: 10 minutes
Cooking time: 5 minutes
Serves: 6

Ingredients To Use:

- 1 stick of soft butter, soft
- ½ cup of sugar
- 12 bread slices
- 1½ tsp vanilla extract
- 1½ tsp cinnamon powder

Step-by-Step Directions to Cook It:

1. Place the cooking pot into the Ninja Foodi Grill and ensure the splatter shield is in position. Close the hood.
2. Press the Bake button. Set the temperature to 400°F and adjust the time to 5 minutes. Press the start/stop button to preheat the appliance for 3 minutes.
3. Mix the sugar, vanilla, soft butter, and cinnamon in a bowl.
4. Spread the butter mix on the bread slice.
5. Arrange the on the cooking pot when the Ninja Foodi Grill is done preheating.
6. Close the hood
7. Serve

Serving suggestions: Serve with freshly squeezed Orange juice

Preparation and Cooking Tips: Leave the slices in the appliance for an extra crispy toast

Nutritional value per serving: Calories: 221kcal, Fat: 4g, Carb: 12g, Proteins: 8g

Creamy Hash Browns

Creamy hash brown is an awesome meal -easy to prepare and a smart choice for breakfast.

Preparation time: 10 minutes
Cooking time: 20 minutes
Serves: 6

Ingredients To Use:

- 2 pounds of hash browns
- 1 cup of whole milk
- 8 bacon slices, diced
- 9 ounces of cream cheese
- 1 yellow onion, sliced
- 1 cup of shredded cheddar cheese
- 6 green onions, sliced
- Salt and black pepper, as desired
- 6 eggs, beaten
- Cooking spray

Step-by-Step Directions to Cook It:

1. Place the cooking pot into the Ninja Foodi Grill and ensure the splatter shield is in position. Close the hood.
2. Press the Bake button. Set the temperature to 350°F and adjust the time to 20 minutes.
3. Press the start/stop button to preheat the appliance for 3 minutes.
4. Mix the eggs, milk, cream cheese, cheddar cheese, onion, bacon, pepper, and salt in a bowl.
5. Add the hash browns to the cooking pot and cover with the egg mix and close the hood.

Serving suggestions: serve immediately

Preparation and Cooking Tips: grease the cooking pot with the cooking spray.

Nutritional value per serving: Calories: 136kcal, Fat: 8g, Carb: 17g, Proteins: 11g

Ninja Biscuit Casserole

Ninja biscuit casserole is satisfying and has a pleasant aroma. Try it now with your Ninja Foodi grill for an amazing delicacy

Preparation time: 10 minutes
Cooking time: 15 minutes
Serves: 8

Ingredients To Use:
- 12 ounces of quartered biscuits
- 3 Tbsp of flour
- ½ pound of chopped sausage
- salt and black pepper, a pinch
- 2½ cups of milk
- Cooking spray

Step-by-Step Directions to Cook It:
1. Place the cooking pot into the Ninja Foodi Grill and ensure the splatter shield is in position. Close the hood.
2. Press the Bake button. Use the default temperature of 350°F and set the time for 15 minutes. Press the start/stop button to preheat the appliance for 3 minutes.
3. Coat a baking pan with the cooking spray.
4. Add the biscuits and sausage.
5. Add the flour, milk, pepper and salt. Mix until well combined
6. Add the baking pan to the preheated Ninja Foodi Grill and close the hood.
7. Divide into 8 portions and serve.

Serving suggestions: Serve with Watermelon Juice

Preparation and Cooking Tips: Press Manual for 2 seconds to check the food's internal temperature

Nutritional value per serving: Calories: 321kcal, Fat: 4g, Carb: 12g, Proteins: 5g

Foodi Hash

Foodi Hash is has a great taste, and with the cheddar topping, the flavor is explosive. Prepared to be blown away.

Preparation time: 10 minutes
Cooking time: 15 minutes
Serves: 6

Ingredients To Use:
- 16 ounces of hash browns
- 2 tbsp of chopped chive
- 1 cup of shredded cheddar
- ½ tsp of paprika
- ½ tsp of garlic powder
- ¼ cup of olive oil
- Salt and black pepper, as desired
- 1 egg, beaten

Step-by-Step Directions to Cook It:
1. Place the cooking pot into the Ninja Foodi Grill and ensure the splatter shield is in position. Close the hood.
2. Press the Bake button. Set the temperature to 350°F and adjust the time to 15 minutes.
3. Press the start/stop button to preheat the appliance for 3 minutes.
4. Add oil to the cooking pot and add the hash browns.
5. Add the paprika, eggs, garlic powder, salt, and pepper.
6. Toss and close the hood.

Serving suggestions: Top with cheddar and serve.
Preparation and Cooking Tips: Use a baking pan rather than the cooking pot for easier cooking
Nutritional value per serving: Calories: 213kcal, Fat: 7g, Carb: 12g, Proteins: 4g

Ninja Oatmeal Casserole

Ninja oatmeal casserole is healthy and tasty. Your diet requirements are fulfilled with this light and delicious meal

Preparation time: 10 minutes
Cooking time: 20 minutes
Serves: 8

Ingredients To Use:
- 2 cups of rolled oats
- ½ cup of chocolate chips
- 1/3 cup of brown sugar
- 1 tsp of cinnamon powder
- 2/3 cup of blueberries
- 1 tsp vanilla extract
- 2 cups of milk
- 1 medium egg
- 2 Tbsp of butter
- 1 tsp of baking powder
- 1 banana, mashed
- Cooking spray

Step-by-Step Directions to Cook It:
1. Place the cooking pot into the Ninja Foodi Grill and ensure the splatter shield is in position. Close the hood.
2. Press the Bake button. Set the temperature to 320°F and adjust the time to 20 minutes. Press the start/stop button to preheat the appliance for 3 minutes.
3. Mix the sugar, cinnamon, baking powder, blueberries, chocolate chips, and banana in a bowl.
4. In another bowl, mix the vanilla extract and eggs with butter.
5. Grease a baking pan with the cooking spray, add the oats mix to the bottom.
6. Layer with the egg mix. Toss.
7. Add the baking pan to the preheated Ninja Foodi Grill and close the hood。 Stir and serve.

Serving suggestions: Serve immediately after cooking
Preparation and Cooking Tips: Use a baking pan rather than the cooking pot of the appliance.
Nutritional value per serving: Calories: 300kcal, Fat: 4g, Carb: 12g, Proteins: 10g

Ninja Bacon Meal

This Ninja Bacon recipe stands apart from other bacon recipes due to the addition of eggs, which give the meal a great taste and pleasant aroma.

Preparation time: 10 minutes
Cooking time: 30 minutes
Serves: 6

Ingredients To Use:
- 8 eggs, beaten
- 1 pound of cubed white bread
- ¼ cup of olive oil
- 1 pound of chopped, smoked, cooked bacon

1 yellow onion, sliced
- ½ tsp of crushed red pepper
- 28 ounces of chopped canned tomatoes

- ½ pound of shredded cheddar
- ½ pound of shredded Monterey jack
- 2 Tbsp of stock
- 2 Tbsp of chopped chives, chopped
- Salt and black pepper, as desired

Step-by-Step Directions to Cook It:

1. Place the cooking pot into the Ninja Foodi Grill and ensure the splatter shield is in position. Close the hood.
2. Press the Bake button. Set the temperature to 350°F and adjust the time to 30 minutes.
3. Press the start/stop button to preheat the appliance for 3 minutes.
4. Add the bread, tomatoes, onion, red pepper, bacon, and stock to the cooking pot.
5. Add the Monterey jack, cheddar, and eggs to the Ninja Foodi Grill and close the hood.

Serving suggestions: Top with chives
Preparation and Cooking Tips: Coat the cooking pot with cooking spray before adding the food.
Nutritional value per serving: Calories: 231kcal, Fat: 5g, Carb: 12g, Proteins: 4g

Ham Breakfast

This recipe has got an amazing taste. It is perfect for mornings that begin with a rush.
Preparation time: 10 minutes
Cooking time: 15 minutes
Serves: 6
Ingredients To Use:

- 6 cups of cubed French bread
- 2 cups of milk
- 10 ounces of cubed ham
- 4 ounces of shredded cheddar cheese
- 1 tbsp mustard
- 5 eggs
- Salt and black pepper, as desired
- 4 ounces of chopped green
- chilies
- Cooking spray

Step-by-Step Directions to Cook It:

1. Place the cooking pot into the Ninja Foodi Grill and ensure the splatter shield is in position. Close the hood.
2. Press the Bake button. Use the default temperature of 350°F and set the time for 15 minutes.
3. Press the start/stop button to preheat the appliance for 3 minutes.
4. Mix the eggs, milk, mustard, cheese, salt, and pepper in a bowl.
5. To the Ninja Foodi Grill's cooking pot, add the bread cubes, ham, and chilies.
6. Add the egg mix, spread over the bread cubes, and close the hood.

Serving suggestions: Serve immediately after cooking
Preparation and Cooking Tips: coat the cooking pot with the cooking spray before adding the bread cubes.
Nutritional value per serving: Calories: 200kcal, Fat: 5g, Carb: 12g, Proteins: 14g

Foodi Fried Eggs

This traditional recipe is transformed with the Ninja Foodi Grill, wich give the eggs a crispy taste.

Preparation time: 10 minutes
Cooking time: 10 minutes
Serves: 2

Ingredients To Use:
- 2 eggs
- 2 Tbsp of butter, melted
- 1 red bell pepper, diced
- sweet paprika, a pinch
- Salt and black pepper, as desired

Step-by-Step Directions to Cook It:
1. Place the cooking pot into the Ninja Foodi Grill and ensure the splatter shield is in position. Close the hood.
2. Press the Bake button. Set the temperature to 140°F and adjust the timer to 10 minutes.
3. Press the start/stop button to preheat the appliance for 3 minutes.
4. Mix the eggs, salt, pepper, paprika, and bell pepper in a bowl.
5. Add the egg mix to the cooking pot of the Ninja Foodi Grill and close the hood.

Serving suggestions: Serve immediately

Preparation and Cooking Tips: The temperature of this meal is very important, do not go against it

Nutritional value per serving: Calories: 200kcal, Fat: 4g, Carb: 10g, Proteins: 3g

Chapter 5: Beef Recipes

Ribeye Steak

Ribeye steak is a delicious and chewy meal that's best served as dinner or lunch.

Preparation time: 10 minutes
Cooking time: 20 minutes
Serves: 4

Ingredients To Use:
- 2 pounds of ribeeye steak
- Salt and black pepper, as desired
- 1 Tbsp of olive oil

For the rub:
- 3 Tbsp sweet paprika
- 1 Tbsp of dried rosemary
- 2 Tbsp onion powder
- 1 Tbsp brown sugar
- 2 Tbsp garlic powder
- 1 Tbsp of ground cumin
- 2 Tbsp of dried oregano

Step-by-Step Directions to Cook It:
1. Place the cooking pot into the Ninja Foodi Grill, and position the grill plate with the handles facing up.
2. Ensure the splatter shield is in position. Close the hood.
3. Press the Grill button. Set the temperature to 400°F and adjust the time to 20 minutes. Press the start/stop button to preheat the appliance for 8 minutes.
4. Mix the paprika, onion, sugar, garlic powder, pepper, salt, rosemary, and cumin to make the rub.
5. Season the ribeye with the rub and coat it with oil.
6. Place the steak on the grill plate and close the hood.

Serving suggestions: Cool for 5 minutes before serving

Preparation and Cooking Tips: Flip the steak during cooking and close the hood to resume cooking.

Nutritional value per serving: Calories: 320kcal, Fat: 8g, Carb: 22g, Proteins: 21g

Steak and Broccoli

Steak and broccoli is an awesome meal that's healthy and great for weight loss. It is tasty and fun to eat.

Preparation time: 45 minutes
Cooking time: 12 minutes
Serves: 4

Ingredients To Use:
- ¾ pound of round steak, stripped
- 1/3 cup of oyster sauce
- 2 tsp of sesame oil
- 1 tsp of sugar
- 1 tsp of soy sauce
- 1 garlic clove, grated
- 1/3 cup of sherry
- 1 pound of broccoli florets, sauteed
- 1 tbsp of olive oil

Step-by-Step Directions to Cook It:
1. Place the cooking pot into the Ninja Foodi Grill, and position the grill plate with the handles facing up. Ensure the splatter shield is in position. Close the hood.

2. Press the Grill button. Set the temperature to 380°F and adjust the time to 12 minutes.
3. Press the start/stop button to preheat the appliance for 8 minutes.
4. Mix the oyster sauce, sesame oil, sherry, soy sauce, and sugar in a bowl
5. Add the beef to the sauce and marinate for 30 minutes.
6. Transfer the flavored beef to the grill plate and season with garlic and oil.
7. Close the hood.
8. Serve with sauteed broccoli

Serving suggestions: Allow steak to cool before serving

Preparation and Cooking Tips: serve with sauteed broccoli

Nutritional value per serving: Calories: 330kcal, Fat: 12g, Carb: 23g, Proteins: 23g

Beef with Onions Marinade

This is a mouth-watering meal that is made exceptional due to the marinade.

Preparation time: 10 minutes
Cooking time: 20 minutes
Serves: 4

Ingredients To Use:
- 1 cup of chopped green onion
- 1 tsp of black pepper
- ½ cup of soy sauce
- 1 pound of lean beef
- ¼ cup of brown sugar
- ¼ cup of sesame seeds
- ½ cup of water
- 5 garlic cloves, grated

Step-by-Step Directions to Cook It:
1. Place the cooking pot into the Ninja Foodi Grill, and position the grill plate with the handles facing up.
2. Ensure the splatter shield is in position. Close the hood.
3. Press the Grill button. Set the temperature to 390°F and adjust the time to 20 minutes.
4. Press the start/stop button to preheat the appliance for 8 minutes.
5. Mix the soy sauce, onion, sugar, garlic, pepper, sesame seed, and water in a bowl
6. Add the meat to the bowl
7. Marinate for 10 minutes
8. Drain the beef.
9. Transfer to the preheated grill plate and close the hood

Serving suggestions: Serve with a side salad

Preparation and Cooking Tips: Press Manual for 2 seconds to check the food's internal temperature

Nutritional value per serving: Calories: 329kcal, Fat: 8g, Carb: 26g, Proteins: 22g

Beef Curry

Beef curry has got great taste. It is healthy and can be enjoyed with other side dishes.

Preparation time: 10 minutes
Cooking time: 45 minutes
Serves: 4

Ingredients To Use:
- 2 pounds of beef steak, quartered

- 3 potatoes, quartered
- 2 Tbsp of olive oil
- 2½ Tbsp of curry powder
- 2 yellow onions, sliced
- 1 Tbsp of wine mustard
- 2 garlic cloves, grated
- 2 Tbsp of tomato sauce
- 10 ounces of canned coconut milk
- Salt and black pepper, as desired

Step-by-Step Directions to Cook It:
1. Place the cooking pot into the Ninja Foodi Grill and ensure the splatter shield is in position. Close the hood.
2. Press the Roast button. Set the temperature to 360°F and adjust the time to 45 minutes.
3. Press the start/stop button to preheat the appliance for 3 minutes.
4. Add the oil, onions, and garlic to the air fryer. Let the timer countdown for 4 minutes.
5. Add the mustard and potato, cook for another 1 minute
6. Add the coconut milk, beef, curry powder, salt, pepper, and tomato sauce.
7. Close the hood and leave to cook for 40 minutes.

Serving suggestions: Serve with a side salad

Preparation and Cooking Tips:
opening the hood stops the cooking, and closing the hood begins the cooking

Nutritional value per serving: Calories: 432kcal, Fat: 16g, Carb: 20g, Proteins: 27g

Foodi Beef Roast

Foodi beef roast is tasty, nutritious and great for lunch or dinner. Try it now with your Ninja Foodi Grill
Preparation time: 10 minutes
Cooking time: 45 minutes
Serves: 6

Ingredients To Use:
- 3 pounds of beef roast
- 3 carrots, sliced
- Salt and black pepper, as desired
- 17 ounces of beef stock
- 5 potatoes, sliced
- 3 ounces of red wine
- ½ tsp of chicken salt
- 1 yellow onion, sliced
- ½ tsp of smoked paprika
- 4 garlic cloves, grated

Step-by-Step Directions to Cook It:
1. Place the cooking pot into the Ninja Foodi Grill, and ensure the splatter shield is in position. Close the hood.
2. Press the Roast button. Set the temperature to 360°F and adjust the time to 45 minutes.
3. Press the start/stop button to preheat the appliance for 3 minutes.
4. Mix the pepper, salt, paprika, chicken salt and rub over the beef.
5. Add the flavored beef to the cooking pot.

6. Add the garlic, stock, wine, carrots, and potatoes.
7. Close the hood

Serving suggestions: Serve with Red Wine

Preparation and Cooking Tips: Press Manual for 2 seconds to check the food's internal temperature

Nutritional value per serving: Calories: 304kcal, Fat: 20g, Carb: 20g, Proteins: 32g

Beef and Cabbage Mix

Beef and cabbage is a fun and tasty meal. It supplies your vegetable requirement, while having an exotic taste.

Preparation time: 10 minutes
Cooking time: 40 minutes
Serves: 6

Ingredients To Use:
- 2½ pounds of beef brisket
- 2 bay leaves
- 1 cup of beef stock
- 3 garlic cloves, sliced
- 1 cabbage head, chopped
- 4 carrots, sliced
- 3 turnips, quartered
- Salt and black pepper, as desired

Step-by-Step Directions to Cook It:
1. Place the cooking pot into the Ninja Foodi Grill, and ensure the splatter shield is in position. Close the hood.
2. Press the Roast button. Set the temperature to 360°F and adjust the time to 40 minutes.

3. Press the start/stop button to preheat the appliance for 3 minutes.
4. Add the beef brisket and stock to the cooking pot.
5. Season with salt and pepper. Add bay leaves, garlic, carrots, potatoes, cabbage, and turnips.
6. Close the hood of the Ninja Foodi Grill

Serving suggestions: Top with raw onions

Preparation and Cooking Tips: Press Manual for 2 seconds to check the food's internal temperature

Nutritional value per serving: Calories: 353kcal, Fat: 16g, Carb: 20g, Proteins: 24g

Worcestershire Beef Roast

The Worcestershire sauce added to this beef roast transforms the taste from regular to extraordinary.

Preparation time: 10 minutes
Cooking time: 1 hour
Serves: 6

Ingredients To Use:
- 4 garlic cloves, grated
- 1 Tbsp Worcestershire sauce
- 1 cup of beef stock
- ½ cup of balsamic vinegar
- 1 Tbsp honey
- 1 medium-sized beef roast
- 1 Tbsp of soy sauce

Step-by-Step Directions to Cook It:
1. Place the cooking pot into the Ninja Foodi Grill, and ensure the splatter shield is in position. Close the hood.

2. Press the Roast button. Set the temperature to 370°F and adjust the time to 1 hour.
3. Press the start/stop button to preheat the appliance for 3 minutes.
4. Coat the beef roast with the Worcestershire sauce, beef stock, honey, garlic, soy sauce, and balsamic vinegar.
5. Transfer the coated beef roast to the cooking pot and close the hood.

Serving suggestions: Serve the sliced-up roast with more Worcestershire sauce

Preparation and Cooking Tips: Flip the beef roast halfway

Nutritional value per serving: Calories: 311kcal, Fat: 7g, Carb: 20g, Proteins: 16g

Foodi Beef Kabobs

Foodi Beef kabob is a tasty meal but can be enjoyed with broccoli and macaroni salad.

Preparation time: 10 minutes
Cooking time: 10 minutes
Serves: 4

Ingredients To Use:
- 2 pounds of cubed sirloin steak
- 2 red bell peppers, sliced
- 1 zucchini, chopped
- 1 red onion, sliced
- 1 lime, juiced
- 2 Tsp of hot sauce
- ½ Tbsp of ground cumin
- ¼ cup of salsa
- 2 Tbsp of chili powder
- ¼ cup of olive oil
- Salt and black pepper, as desired

Step-by-Step Directions to Cook It:
1. Place the cooking pot into the Ninja Foodi Grill, and position the grill plate with the handles facing up.
2. Ensure the splatter shield is in position. Close the hood.
3. Press the Grill button. Set the temperature to 370°F and adjust the time to 10 minutes.
4. Press the start/stop button to preheat the appliance for 8 minutes.
5. Mix the lime juice, salsa, chili powder, hot sauce, black pepper, salt, oil, and cumin in a bowl- for the rub
6. Arrange the meat, sliced bell peppers, onions, and zucchini, on skewers.
7. Brush the kabobs with the rub until well coated.
8. Transfer the kabobs to the grill plate and close the hood.

Serving suggestions: Serve with a side salad

Preparation and Cooking Tips: Flip Kabobs halfway

Nutritional value per serving: Calories: 170kcal, Fat: 5g, Carb: 13g, Proteins: 16g

Mexican Beef Roast

Mexican beef roast has an attractive aroma that is sure to have the neighbors knocking on your door for the recipe

Preparation time: 10 minutes
Cooking time: 70 minutes
Serves: 8

Ingredients To Use:
- 2 yellow onions, sliced
- ½ cup of pitted and chopped black olives
- 2 Tbsp of olive oil
- 2 green bell peppers, sliced
- 2 pounds of cubed beef roast
- habanero pepper, sliced
- 14 ounces canned tomatoes, sliced
- 4 jalapenos, sliced
- 2 Tbsp of cilantro, sliced
- 6 garlic cloves, grated
- Salt and black pepper, as desired
- ½ cup of water
- 1 tsp of dried oregano
- 1½ tsp of ground cumin

Step-by-Step Directions to Cook It:
1. Place the cooking pot into the Ninja Foodi Grill, and position the grill plate with the handles facing up.
2. Ensure the splatter shield is in position. Close the hood.
3. Press the Grill button. Set the temperature to 300°F and adjust the time to 10 minutes.
4. Press the start/stop button to preheat the appliance for 8 minutes.
5. Mix the cubed beef with the oil, habanero, garlic, tomatoes, cilantro, cumin, pepper, salt, oregano, onions, jalapenos, and water.
6. Transfer the coated beef to the grill plate and close the hood.

Serving suggestions: Top with olives
Preparation and Cooking Tips: Stir the beef regularly while cooking
Nutritional value per serving: Calories: 305kcal, Fat: 14g, Carb: 18g, Proteins: 25g

Ninja Beef Casserole

Ninja Beef casserole is a delightful and healthy meal. It contains beneficial nutrients and is diet friendly
Preparation time: 30 minutes
Cooking time: 35 minutes
Serves: 12

Ingredients To Use:
- 1 Tbsp of olive oil
- 1 tsp of dried oregano
- 2 pounds of ground beef
- Salt and black pepper, as desired
- 2 tsp of mustard
- 2 cups of chopped eggplant
- 2 tsp of gluten-free Worcestershire sauce
- 28 ounces of chopped canned tomatoes
- 16 ounces of tomato sauce
- 2 cups of grated mozzarella
- 2 Tbsp of chopped parsley

Step-by-Step Directions to Cook It:
1. Place the cooking pot into the Ninja Foodi Grill and ensure the splatter shield is in position. Close the hood.
2. Press the Bake button. Set the temperature to 360°F and adjust the time to 35 minutes.
3. Press the start/stop button to preheat the appliance for 3 minutes.

4. Mix the eggplant, oil, pepper, and salt in a bowl.
5. In a separate bowl, mix the beef, mustard, Worcestershire sauce, pepper, and salt.
6. Spread the beef mix on the cooking pot.
7. Layer the beef mix with the eggplant mix.
8. Top with the tomatoes, parsley, oregano, tomato sauce. Drizzle with the mozzarella. Close the hood.

Serving suggestions: Serve immediately

Preparation and Cooking Tips: Ensure the beef mix is evenly spread for consistent cooking

Nutritional value per serving: Calories: 200kcal, Fat: 12g, Carb: 16g, Proteins: 15g

Chapter 6: Pork Recipes

Foodi Grilled Pork

Foodi grilled pork is grilled to perfection with the Ninja Foodi Grill. Try it now for a delightful meal
Preparation time: 10 minutes
Cooking time: 22 minutes
Serves: 6
Ingredients To Use:
- 2 pounds of boneless, cubed pork meat
- 2 yellow onions, diced
- 1 tbsp olive oil
- 1 garlic clove, grated
- 3 cups of chicken stock
- 2 Tbsp of sweet paprika
- Salt and black pepper, as desired
- 2 Tbsp of white flour
- 1½ cups sour cream
- 2 Tbsp of chopped dill
Step-by-Step Directions to Cook It:
1. Place the cooking pot into the Ninja Foodi Grill, and position the grill plate with the handles facing up.
2. Ensure the splatter shield is in position. Close the hood.
3. Press the Grill button. Set the temperature to 370°F and adjust the time to 23 minutes.
4. Press the start/stop button to preheat the appliance for 8 minutes.
5. Season the pork with salt and pepper. Rub with oil

6. Transfer the pork to the grill plate and cook for 7 minutes, flipping halfway.
7. When the timer countdown to 15 minutes, add the onions, garlic, flour, paprika, sour cream, and dill.
8. Serve.
Serving suggestions: Serve after 5 minutes
Preparation and Cooking Tips: Press Manual for 2 seconds to check the food's internal temperature
Nutritional value per serving: Calories: 300kcal, Fat: 4g, Carb: 26g, Proteins: 34g

Herbed Pork Roast

Herbed pork roast is a delicacy that can be prepared for Thanksgiving and other festivities. The pork is easy to chew and melts on the tongue.
Preparation time: 10 minutes
Cooking time: 15 minutes
Serves: 2
Ingredients To Use:
- 1 red onion, chopped
- 7 ounces of pork tenderloin
- 1 yellow bell pepper, sliced
- ½ Tbsp of mustard
- 1 green bell pepper, sliced
- 2 tsp of Provencal herbs
- 1 Tbsp of olive oil
- Salt and black pepper, as desired
Step-by-Step Directions to Cook It:

1. Place the cooking pot into the Ninja Foodi Grill and ensure the splatter shield is in position. Close the hood.
2. Press the Roast button. Set the temperature to 370°F and adjust the time to 15 minutes.
3. Press the start/stop button to preheat the appliance for 3 minutes.
4. Combine the yellow bell pepper, green bell pepper, salt, pepper, onion, ½ oil, and Provencal herbs in a bowl.
5. Season the pork with salt, pepper, and rub with the rest of the oil.
6. Transfer the pork and bell pepper mix to the cooking pot and close the hood.

Serving suggestions: Serve pork with bell pepper as side dish

Preparation and Cooking Tips: Flip the pork and stir the veggies halfway

Nutritional value per serving: Calories: 300kcal, Fat: 8g, Carb: 21g, Proteins: 23g

Tasty Pork Chops

Tasty pork chops are delightful and exciting to the taste bud; it is best taken when in a celebratory mood
Preparation time: 24 hours
Cooking time: 25 minutes
Serves: 6
Ingredients To Use:
- 2 pork chops
- ¼ cup of olive oil
- 2 yellow onions, chopped
- 2 garlic cloves, grated
- 2 tsp of mustard

- 1 tsp of sweet paprika
- Salt and black pepper, as desired
- ½ tsp dried oregano
- ½ tsp of dried thyme
- cayenne pepper, a pinch

Step-by-Step Directions to Cook It:
1. Mix the oil, garlic, paprika, mustard, oregano, thyme, cayenne, and black pepper in a bowl.
2. Coat the meat with the mustard mix and combine with the onions. Marinate and keep in the fridge for 24 hours
3. Place the cooking pot into the Ninja Foodi Grill, then the crisper basket. Ensure the splatter shield is in position and close the hood.
4. Press the air crisp button. Set the temperature to 360°F and set the time for 25 minutes.
5. Press the start/stop button to preheat the appliance for 3 minutes.
6. Transfer the pork to the crisper basket and close the hood.

Serving suggestions: Serve with Salad
Preparation and Cooking Tips:
Discard the marinade onions
Nutritional value per serving: Calories: 384kcal, Fat: 4g, Carb: 17g, Proteins: 25g

Pork with Wild Rice

Pork with wild rice is an exciting meal; it is fun to eat and provides the body with vital nutrients.
Preparation time: 10 minutes
Cooking time: 35 minutes
Serves: 6

Ingredients To Use:

- 2½ pounds of boneless and trimmed pork loin
- 2 cups of cooked wild rice
- ¾ cup of chicken stock
- 1 tsp of dried basil
- 2 Tbsp of olive oil
- 2¼ tsp of dried sage
- ½ Tbsp of garlic powder
- ½ Tbsp of sweet paprika
- ¼ tsp of dried rosemary
- ¼ tsp of dried marjoram
- 1 tsp of dried oregano
- Salt and black pepper, as desired

Step-by-Step Directions to Cook It:

1. Place the cooking pot into the Ninja Foodi Grill and ensure the splatter shield is in position. Close the hood.
2. Press the Bake button. Use the default temperature of 375°F and set the time for 35 minutes.
3. Press the start/stop button to preheat the appliance for 3 minutes.
4. Mix the paprika, stock, sage, garlic powder, rosemary, marjoram, thyme, salt, pepper, and oregano in a bowl.
5. Add the pork loin to the stick mix and marinate for one hour.
6. Transfer the pork and marinade to the cooking pot and close the hood.

Serving suggestions: Serve with the wild rice

Preparation and Cooking Tips: Stir the food regularly

Nutritional value per serving: Calories: 310kcal, Fat: 4g, Carb: 37g, Proteins: 34g

Air-Crisped Pork Shoulder

Air-Crisped shoulder pork is a heavy but refreshing meal. Great for lunch or dinner on a stressful day. It will replenish your depleted energy
Preparation time: 30 minutes
Cooking time: 1 hour 20 minutes
Serves: 6

Ingredients To Use:

- 3 Tbsp of minced garlic
- 3 Tbsp of olive oil
- 4 pounds of pork shoulder
- Salt and black pepper, as desired

Step-by-Step Directions to Cook It:

1. Place the cooking pot into the Ninja Foodi Grill, then the crisper basket. Ensure the splatter shield is in position and close the hood.
2. Press the air crisp button. Set the temperature to 390°F and set the time for 10 minutes.
3. Press the start/stop button to preheat the appliance for 3 minutes.
4. Mix all the ingredients besides the pork in a bowl.
5. Coat both sides of the pork with the mix and transfer to the crisper basket.
6. Close the hood.
7. Press the roast button, change the temperature to 300°, and set the timer for 1 hour 10 minutes.

Serving suggestions: Carve and serve with salad

Preparation and Cooking Tips: Flip the pork halfway

Nutritional value per serving: Calories: 221kcal, Fat: 4g, Carb: 7g, Proteins: 10g

Foodi Roasted Pork belly with Special Sauce

Try this recipe out for a truly remarkable meal. With the sauce, the pork is juicy and delicious.

Preparation time: 10 minutes
Cooking time: 40 minutes
Serves: 6

Ingredients To Use:
- 2 Tbsp of sugar
- 1 tsp of olive oil
- 1 Tbsp of lemon juice
- 17 ounces of apples, cored and wedged
- 1 quart of water
- 2 pounds of scored pork belly
- Salt and black pepper, as desired

Step-by-Step Directions to Cook It:
1. Place the cooking pot into the Ninja Foodi Grill, and ensure the splatter shield is in position. Close the hood.
2. Press the Roast button. Set the temperature to 400°F and adjust the time to 40 minutes.
3. Press the start/stop button to preheat the appliance for 3 minutes.
4. Blend the apples, lemon juice, sugar, and water.
5. Transfer the blended juice to a bowl and add the meat.
6. After thoroughly coating the meat, transfer to the cooking pot and close the hood.
7. After the pork is done cooking, remove from the air fryer and pour the leftover blended juice into the pot and increase the timer by 15 minutes

Serving suggestions: Serve the pork with special Apple sauce
Preparation and Cooking Tips: Flip the pork halfway
Nutritional value per serving: Calories: 456kcal, Fat: 34g, Carb: 10g, Proteins: 25g

Foodi Stuffed Pork

Stuffed pork is an awesome meal that requires minimal expertise. Just bring out your Ninja Foodi grill and start cooking.

Preparation time: 10 minutes
Cooking time: 20 minutes
Serves: 4

Ingredients To Use:
- 2 limes, juiced, zested, and grated
- 2 Tbsp of mustard
- 1 orange, juiced, zested, and grated
- 6 Swiss cheese slices
- 4 tsp of minced garlic,
- ¾ cup of olive oil
- 4 ham slices
- 1 cup of chopped cilantro
- 2 pickles, sliced
- 1 cup of chopped mint
- 1 tsp of dried oregano
- 4 pork loin steaks
- Salt and black pepper, as desired
- 2 tsp of ground cumin

Step-by-Step Directions to Cook It:

1. Place the cooking pot into the Ninja Foodi Grill, and position the grill plate with the handles facing up.
2. Ensure the splatter shield is in position. Close the hood.
3. Press the Grill button. Set the temperature to 340°F and adjust the time to 20 minutes.
4. Blend the lime zest, orange zest, orange juice, lime juice, oil, garlic, cilantro, oregano, mint, salt, pepper, and cumin in a food processor. Pulse until smooth.
5. Season the pork steaks with pepper and salt.
6. Transfer the blended marinade to a bowl and add the pork steaks. Toss until well coated.
7. Arrange the steaks on a flat surface.
8. On each steak, add a slice of ham, cheese, some pickles, and mustard. Roll the pork steaks and secure them with toothpicks.
9. Transfer the stuffed pork to the grill plate and close the hood.

Serving suggestions: Serve with salad

Preparation and Cooking Tips: Flip the pork halfway

Nutritional value per serving: Calories: 270kcal, Fat: 7g, Carb: 13g, Proteins: 20g

Mushroom Pork Chops

This is an exceptional recipe for mushroom lovers. It combines the unique taste and pork to produce a delightful meal

Preparation time: 10 minutes
Cooking time: 40 minutes

Serves: 3

Ingredients To Use:
- 8 ounces of chopped mushrooms
- 1 tsp of garlic powder
- 1 yellow onion, sliced
- 1 cup of mayonnaise
- 3 pork chops,
- 1 tsp of nutmeg
- 1 Tbsp of balsamic vinegar
- ½ cup of olive oil

Step-by-Step Directions to Cook It:
1. Place the cooking pot into the Ninja Foodi Grill, and ensure the splatter shield is in position. Close the hood.
2. Press the Bake button. Set the temperature to 330°F and adjust the time to 30 minutes.
3. Press the start/stop button to preheat the appliance for 3 minutes.
4. Grease the cooking pot with the oil and add the onions and mushroom.
5. Season the pork chops with garlic powder and nutmeg.
6. Add the seasoned pork to the air fryer and close the hood.

Serving suggestions: Drizzle the vinegar and mayo over the pork

Preparation and Cooking Tips: Flip the pork halfway

Nutritional value per serving: Calories: 600kcal, Fat: 10g, Carb: 8g, Proteins: 30g

Coffee Flavored Pork Steak

Coffee flavored pork steak is a tasty meal that is tailored for meat lovers

and caffeine enthusiasts. The taste is simply amazing.

Preparation time: 10 minutes
Cooking time: 15 minutes
Serves: 4

Ingredients To Use:
- 1½ Tbsp of ground coffee
- 4 pounds of pork tenderloin
- Black pepper, as desired
- ½ Tbsp of sweet paprika
- 2 tsp of garlic powder
- 2 Tbsp of chili powder
- 2 tsp of onion powder
- ¼ tsp of ground coriander
- ¼ tsp of ground ginger
- cayenne pepper, as desired

Step-by-Step Directions to Cook It:
1.   Place the cooking pot into the Ninja Foodi Grill, and position the grill plate with the handles facing up.
2.   Ensure the splatter shield is in position. Close the hood.
3.   Press the Grill button. Set the temperature to 360°F and adjust the time to 15 minutes.
4.   Mix the coffee, paprika, chili powder, garlic powder, onion powder, coriander, ginger, black pepper, and coriander in a bowl.
5.   Coat both sides of the steak with the coffee mix.
6.   Transfer the steak to the grill plate and close the hood.
7.   Divide the pork into 4 portions

Serving suggestions: Serve with salad
Preparation and Cooking Tips: Flip the steak halfway
Nutritional value per serving: Calories: 160kcal, Fat: 10g, Carb: 14g, Proteins: 12g

Roasted Pork Chops and Peppers

Roasted pork chops and pepper is an amazing meal that packs no punch. The spice is mild, and the veggies are a delightful addition.

Preparation time: 10 minutes
Cooking time: 16 minutes
Serves: 4

Ingredients To Use:
- 3 Tbsp of olive oil
- 2 roasted bell peppers, sliced
- 3 Tbsp of lemon juice
- 2 Tbsp of chopped thyme
- 3 garlic cloves, grated
- 1 Tbsp of smoked paprika
- 4 pork chops,
- Salta and black pepper, as desired

Step-by-Step Directions to Cook It:
1.   Place the cooking pot into the Ninja Foodi Grill, and ensure the splatter shield is in position. Close the hood.
2.   Press the Roast button. Set the temperature to 400°F and adjust the time to 16 minutes.
3.   Press the start/stop button to preheat the appliance for 3 minutes.
4.   Rub the pork chops with lemon juice, oil, paprika, garlic, thyme, salt, bell peppers, black pepper, and salt.
5.   Transfer the seasoned pork to the cooking pot and close the hood.

Serving suggestions: Serve with salad
Preparation and Cooking Tips: Flip the pork halfway
Nutritional value per serving: Calories: 321kcal, Fat: 6g, Carb: 14g, Proteins: 17g

Chapter 7: Lamb Recipes

Lamb Chops

With the Ninja Foodi Grill, this meal is transformed into an exceptional delicacy. Try it out now.
Preparation time: 10 minutes
Cooking time: 10 minutes
Serves: 4

Ingredients To Use:
- 3 Tbsp olive oil
- 8 lamb chops
- Salt and black pepper, as desired
- 4 garlic cloves, grated
- 1 Tbsp of chopped oregano
- 1 Tbsp of chopped coriander

Step-by-Step Directions to Cook It:
1. Place the cooking pot into the Ninja Foodi Grill, and position the grill plate with the handles facing up. Ensure the splatter shield is in position. Close the hood.
2. Press the Grill button. Set the temperature to 400°F and adjust the time to 10 minutes. Press the start/stop button to preheat the appliance for 8 minutes.
3. Mix the oregano, pepper, salt, garlic, and oil in a small bowl.
4. Rub the oregano mix on the lamb chops
5. Place the lamb chops on the grill plate and close the hood.

Serving suggestions: Serve after 5 minutes to allow steak cool appropriately before consumption
Preparation and Cooking Tips: Press Manual for 2 seconds to check the food's internal temperature
Nutritional value per serving: Calories: 213kcal, Fat: 7g, Carb: 14g, Proteins: 23g

Lamb Potatoes Roast

Lamb potatoes roast is an amazing meal. It is highly nutritious and tasty.
Preparation time: 10 minutes
Cooking time: 45 minutes
Serves: 6

Ingredients To Use:
- 4 pounds of lamb roast
- 4 bay leaves
- 1 spring rosemary
- 6 potatoes, cut into halves
- 3 garlic cloves, grated
- ½ cup of lamb stock
- Salt and black pepper, as desired

Step-by-Step Directions to Cook It:
6. Place the cooking pot into the Ninja Foodi Grill, and ensure the splatter shield is in position. Close the hood.
7. Press the Roast button. Set the temperature to 360°F and adjust the time to 45 minutes.
8. Press the start/stop button to preheat the appliance for 3 minutes.

9. Add the potatoes to the cooking pot.
10. Add the lamb, rosemary spring, garlic, pepper, salt, stock, and bay leaves.
11. Toss and close the hood.

Serving suggestions: Slice the lamb, and serve with potatoes and cooking juice
Preparation and Cooking Tips: stir and flip the lamb halfway for consistent cooking
Nutritional value per serving: Calories: 273kcal, Fat: 4g, Carb: 25g, Proteins: 29g

Ninja Air-Fried Lamb Shanks

Ninja Air-Fried lamb shanks is a tasty meal that will excite your taste bud. It is nutritious and fun to eat.
Preparation time: 10 minutes
Cooking time: 45 minutes
Serves: 4
Ingredients To Use:
- 4 lamb shanks
- 2 tsp honey
- 1 Tbsp olive oil
- 2 Tbsp white flour
- 1 yellow onion, sliced
- 4 bay leaves
- 5 ounces of dry sherry
- 4 Tbsp coriander seeds, crushed
- Salt and pepper, as desired
- 2½ cups of chicken stock

Step-by-Step Directions to Cook It:
1. Place the cooking pot into the Ninja Foodi Grill, and position the grill plate with the handles facing up.
2. Ensure the splatter shield is in position. Close the hood.
3. Press the Grill button. Set the temperature to 360°F and adjust the time to 10 minutes.
4. Press the start/stop button to preheat the appliance for 8 minutes.
5. Season the lamb shanks with salt and pepper.
6. Rub the shanks with oil, and transfer to the preheated air fryer.
7. Carefully remove the grill pan and add the rest of the oil to the cooking pan.
8. Add the onion, coriander and increase the timer by 5 minutes.
9. Add the flour, honey, bay leaves, sherry, stock, salt, and pepper to the cooking pot.
10. Add the lamb and increase the timer by 30 minutes.

Serving suggestions: Serve after 5 minutes
Preparation and Cooking Tips: Press Manual for 2 seconds to check the food's internal temperature
Nutritional value per serving: Calories: 283kcal, Fat: 4g, Carb: 17g, Proteins: 26g

Ninja Lemon Lamb

Lemon lamb roast is a chewy and tasty meal. It is fun to eat; it provides the body with necessary nutrients.
Preparation time: 10 minutes
Cooking time: 30 minutes
Serves: 4
Ingredients To Use:
- 2 lamb shanks
- ½ tsp of dried oregano

- 2 garlic cloves, grated
- 4 Tbsp of olive oil
- ½ lemon, juiced and zested
- Salt and black pepper, as desired

Step-by-Step Directions to Cook It:

1. Place the cooking pot into the Ninja Foodi Grill, and ensure the splatter shield is in position. Close the hood.
2. Press the Roast button. Set the temperature to 350°F and adjust the time to 30 minutes.
3. Press the start/stop button to preheat the appliance for 3 minutes.
4. Season the lamb with black pepper, salt, and garlic.
5. Transfer to the air fryer and close the hood.
6. Mix the zest and lemon juice in a bowl. Drizzle with salt, pepper, oregano, and olive oil. Stir thoroughly.

Serving suggestions: Shred up the roasted lamb and drizzle with the lemon dressing

Preparation and Cooking Tips: Flip the lamb halfway

Nutritional value per serving: Calories: 260kcal, Fat: 7g, Carb: 15g, Proteins: 12g

Fennel Lamb Rack

Fennel lamb rack is a tasty meal which gives nutrient to the body. It is best served as lunch or dinner.

Preparation time: 10 minutes
Cooking time: 16 minutes
Serves: 4

Ingredients To Use:

- 12 ounces of lamb racks

- 1 Tbsp of brown sugar
- 2 fennel bulbs, chopped
- 2 Tbsp of olive oil
- 4 figs, halved
- Salt and black pepper, as desired
- 1/8 cup of apple cider vinegar

Step-by-Step Directions to Cook It:

1. Place the cooking pot into the Ninja Foodi Grill, and ensure the splatter shield is in position. Close the hood.
2. Press the Bake button. Set the temperature to 350°F and adjust the time to 6 minutes.
3. Press the start/stop button to preheat the appliance for 3 minutes.
4. Mix the figs, fennel, vinegar, oil, and sugar in a baking pan and transfer to the air fryer.
5. Close the hood.
6. Season the lamb with pepper and salt.
7. Replace the baking pan with the crisper basket.
8. Close the hood, press the air crisp button, and set the time for 10 minutes at 350°F.
9. Press the start button, then add the seasoned lamb when the appliance displays "ADD FOOD."

Serving suggestions: Serve the crisp lamb with the baked vegetables

Preparation and Cooking Tips: Flip the lamb halfway

Nutritional value per serving: Calories: 240kcal, Fat: 9g, Carb: 15g, Proteins: 12g

Air-Crisped Lamb Ribs

With the Ninja Foodi Grill's air-crisp function, the ribs are cooked to perfection. The meat is chewy, moist, and delicious.
Preparation time: 15 minutes
Cooking time: 40 minutes
Serves: 8

Ingredients To Use:
- 4 garlic cloves, grated
- 8 lamb ribs
- 2 carrots, diced
- 2 Tbsp of extra virgin olive oil
- Salt and black pepper, as desired
- 1 Tbsp of chopped rosemary
- 1 cup of veggie stock
- 3 Tbsp of white flour

Step-by-Step Directions to Cook It:
1. Place the cooking pot and crisper basket into the Ninja Foodi Grill, and ensure the splatter shield is in position. Close the hood.
2. Press the Air Crisp button. Set the temperature to 360°F and adjust the time to 10 minutes.
3. Press the start/stop button to preheat the appliance for 3 minutes.
4. Season the ribs with pepper and salt.
5. Coat ribs with oil and garlic.
6. Transfer to the crisper basket and close the hood.
7. Mix the flour, veggie stock, and rosemary in a bowl.
8. Coat both sides of the lamb with the flour mix and top with the carrots.
9. Increase the timer by 30 minutes
Serving suggestions: Serve hot

Preparation and Cooking Tips: Flip Lamb regularly
Nutritional value per serving: Calories: 302kcal, Fat: 7g, Carb: 22g, Proteins: 27g

Ninja Foodi Signature Air-Crisped Lamb

Air-crisped lamb is a chewy and crispy meal that can serve many purposes. Try it out on your Ninja Foodi Grill for a true delicacy
Preparation time: 10 minutes
Cooking time: 42 minutes
Serves: 8

Ingredients To Use:
- 2½ pounds of chopped lamb shoulder
- 3 Tbsp of honey
- 3 ounces of peeled and chopped almonds
- 9 ounces of pitted plumps
- 8 ounces of veggie stock
- 2 yellow onions, sliced
- 2 garlic cloves, grated
- Salt and black pepper, as desired
- 1 tsp of cumin powder
- 1 tsp of turmeric powder
- 1 tsp of ginger powder
- 1 tsp of cinnamon powder
- 3 Tbsp olive oil

Step-by-Step Directions to Cook It:
1. Place the cooking pot into the Ninja Foodi Grill, then the crisper basket. Ensure the splatter shield is in position and close the hood.
2. Press the air crisp button. Set the temperature to 350°F and set the time for 8 minutes.

3. Press the start/stop button to preheat the appliance for 3 minutes.
4. Mix the olive oil, ginger, turmeric, cumin, and garlic in a bowl.
5. Coat the lamb with the garlic mix and transfer to the crisper basket
6. Remove the crisper basket and transfer the lamb, stock, onions, plums, and honey to the cooking pot.
7. Increase the timer by 35 minutes

Serving suggestions: Top with almonds

Preparation and Cooking Tips: Follow the recommendations fastidiously

Nutritional value per serving: Calories: 432kcal, Fat: 23g, Carb: 30g, Proteins: 20g

Foodi Short Ribs with Sauce

Short ribs with sauce are delightful and mouth-watering. It is best enjoyed as dinner.

Preparation time: 10 minutes
Cooking time: 36 minutes
Serves: 4

Ingredients To Use:
- 2 green onions, chopped
- 1 tsp of vegetable oil
- 3 garlic cloves, minced
- 3 ginger slices
- 4 pounds of short ribs
- ½ cup water
- ½ cup soy sauce
- ¼ cup rice wine
- ¼ cup pear juice
- 2 tsp of sesame oil

Step-by-Step Directions to Cook It:
1. Place the cooking pot into the Ninja Foodi Grill and ensure the splatter shield is in position. Close the hood.
2. Press the Bake button. Use the default temperature of 350°F and set the time for 35 minutes.
3. Press the start/stop button to preheat the appliance for 3 minutes.
4. Grease the cooking pot with the oil, add the green onions, garlic, and ginger.
5. Add the water, wine, sesame oil, soy sauce, pear juice, and ribs.
6. Close the hood

Serving suggestions: Cut up the ribs and drizzle with the sauce

Preparation and Cooking Tips: Flip the ribs regularly

Nutritional value per serving: Calories: 321kcal, Fat: 12g, Carb: 20g, Proteins: 14g

Citrus Lamb

Citrus lamb is a great meal. It is nutritious; it provides the body with various vital nutrients.

Preparation time: 60 minutes
Cooking time: 45 minutes
Serves: 4

Ingredients To Use:
- 1 cup of parsley
- 1 orange, juiced
- 1 cup of mint
- 1 small yellow onion, chopped
- 1/3 cup of chopped pistachios
- 5 Tbsp of olive oil
- 1 tsp of lemon zest, grated
- Salt and black pepper, as desired
- ½ onion, chopped
- 2 pounds of lamb riblets

- 5 garlic cloves, grated

Step-by-Step Directions to Cook It:

1. Place the cooking pot into the Ninja Foodi Grill and ensure the splatter shield is in position. Close the hood.
2. Press the Bake button. Use the default temperature of 300°F and set the time for 45 minutes.
3. Press the start/stop button to preheat the appliance for 3 minutes.
4. Blend the parsley, onion, mint, pistachios, salt, pepper, lemon zest, and oil in a food processor.
5. Coat the lamb with the lemon mix and marinate for an hour.
6. Transfer the lamb to the cooking pot, drizzle with orange juice, sprinkle with garlic, and close the hood.

Serving suggestions: Serve after 5 minutes

Preparation and Cooking Tips: Flip the lamb halfway

Nutritional value per serving: Calories: 200kcal, Fat: 4g, Carb: 15g, Proteins: 7g

Lamb with Veggies

Lamb with veggies is an amazing meal. It provides the body with essential nutrients. It includes veggies into your meal. It is mouth-watering and fun to eat.

Preparation time: 10 minutes
Cooking time: 30 minutes
Serves: 4

Ingredients To Use:

- 8 ounces of sliced lamb loin
- 1 carrot, diced
- ½ Tbsp of olive oil
- 1 onion, chopped
- 3 ounces of bean sprouts

For the marinade:

- ½ apple, minced
- 1 garlic clove, grated
- 1 small yellow onion, minced
- 5 Tbsp of soy sauce
- 1 Tbsp ginger, minced
- 1 Tbsp of sugar
- Salt and black pepper, as desired
- 2 Tbsp of orange juice

Step-by-Step Directions to Cook It:

1. Place the cooking pot into the Ninja Foodi Grill and ensure the splatter shield is in position. Close the hood.
2. Press the Bake button. Use the default temperature of 360°F and set the time for 25 minutes.
3. Press the start/stop button to preheat the appliance for 3 minutes.
4. Combine the marinade ingredients in a bowl.
5. Coat the lamb with the marinade and set aside for 10 minutes
6. Coat the cooking pot with the olive oil and add the onion, bean sprouts, and carrots.
7. Add the lamb and drizzle with the marinade.
8. Close the hood.

Serving suggestions: Slice the lamb and serve with the cooked marinade

Preparation and Cooking Tips: Flip the lamb halfway

Chapter 8: Chicken and Turkey Recipes

Foodi Coconut Chicken

Coconut chicken is a savory meal; it excites the taste bud and pleasures the senses
Preparation time: 120 minutes
Cooking time: 25 minutes
Serves: 4
Ingredients To Use:
- 4 drumsticks
- 5 tsp of turmeric powder
- 2 Tbsp of grated ginger
- Salt and black pepper, as desired
- 4 Tbsp of coconut cream

Step-by-Step Directions to Cook It:
1. Place the cooking pot into the Ninja Foodi Grill, then the crisper basket. Ensure the splatter shield is in position and close the hood.
2. Press the air crisp button. Set the temperature to 370°F and set the time for 25 minutes.
3. Press the start/stop button to preheat the appliance for 3 minutes.
4. Mix the turmeric, cream, ginger, pepper, and salt in a bowl.
5. Add the chicken to the bowl and toss.
6. Transfer the drumsticks to the crisper basket and close the hood.

Serving suggestions: Serve with a side salad
Preparation and Cooking Tips: Follow the temperature and time instructions for the best crispy taste

Nutritional value per serving: Calories: 300kcal, Fat: 4g, Carb: 22g, Proteins: 20g

Chinese Wings

This is a great recipe for a traditional meal. The resulting chicken wings are delicious, nutritious, juicy, and chewy.
Preparation time: 120 minutes
Cooking time: 15 minutes
Serves: 6
Ingredients To Use:
- 16 chicken wings
- 3 Tbsp of lime juice
- 2 Tbsp of honey
- 2 Tbsp of soy sauce
- ¼ tsp of white pepper
- Salt and black pepper, as desired

Step-by-Step Directions to Cook It:
1. Place the cooking pot into the Ninja Foodi Grill, then the crisper basket. Ensure the splatter shield is in position and close the hood.
2. Press the air crisp button. Set the temperature to 370°F and set the time for 12 minutes.
3. Press the start/stop button to preheat the appliance for 3 minutes.
4. Mix the honey, soy sauce, white and black pepper, lime juice, and salt in a bowl.
5. Add the chicken wings.
6. Transfer to the crisper basket.
7. Close the hood.
8. For additional crispiness, press the Broil button, set the temperature

to 400°, and timer for 3 more minutes. This is only available to the Ninja Foodi Smart XL model.

Serving suggestions: Serve immediately

Preparation and Cooking Tips: Flip the food halfway for consistent cooking.

Nutritional value per serving: Calories: 372kcal, Fat: 9g, Carb: 37g, Proteins: 24g

Spiced Whole Chicken

Spiced whole chicken is a fantastic meal. A premium recipe reserved for special occasions.

Preparation time: 30 minutes
Cooking time: 40 minutes
Serves: 4

Ingredients To Use:
- 1 whole chicken (small-sized)
- 2 Tbsp of olive oil
- Salt and black pepper, as desired
- 1 tsp of garlic powder
- ½ tsp of dried thyme
- 1 tsp of onion powder
- 1 tsp of dried rosemary
- 1 Tbsp of lemon juice

Step-by-Step Directions to Cook It:
1. Place the cooking pot into the Ninja Foodi Grill, then the crisper basket. Ensure the splatter shield is in position and close the hood.
2. Press the air crisp button. Set the temperature to 360°F and set the time for 40 minutes.
3. Press the start/stop button to preheat the appliance for 3 minutes.

4. Mix the lemon juice, salt, pepper, onion powder, rosemary, thyme, and garlic powder in a bowl.
5. Thoroughly coat the chicken with lemon mix and olive oil. Marinate for 30 minutes.
6. Transfer the chicken to the crisper basket.

Serving suggestions: Carve and serve with salad

Preparation and Cooking Tips: Flip the chicken regularly

Nutritional value per serving: Calories: 390kcal, Fat: 10g, Carb: 22g, Proteins: 20g

Foodi Air-Crisped Chicken Breast

The air crisp function of the Ninja Foodi Grill always produces incredible meals, and this is no exception.

Preparation time: 10 minutes
Cooking time: 20 minutes
Serves: 4

Ingredients To Use:
- 16 ounces of Salsa Verde
- 1 tsp garlic powder
- 1 Tbsp of olive oil
- 1 pound of boneless and skinless chicken breast
- 1½ cup of grated Monterey Jack cheese
- Salt and black pepper, as desired
- ¼ cup of chopped cilantro

Step-by-Step Directions to Cook It:
1. Place the cooking pot into the Ninja Foodi Grill and ensure the splatter shield is in position. Close the hood.

2. Press the Bake button. Use the default temperature of 380°F and set the time for 20 minutes.
3. Press the start/stop button to preheat the appliance for 3 minutes.
4. Season the chicken with black pepper, salt, garlic powder, and olive oil.
5. Pour the Salsa Verde into the cooking pot and arrange the seasoned chicken breasts in it.
6. Close the hood.
7. After 18 minutes, top the chicken breast with the cheese

Serving suggestions: Serve with salad
Preparation and Cooking Tips: Flip the chicken regularly
Nutritional value per serving: Calories: 340kcal, Fat: 18g, Carb: 32g, Proteins: 18g

Ninja Duck Breasts

Duck breast is nutritious and tasty. It has a soft, chewy taste.
Preparation time: 10 minutes
Cooking time: 22 minutes
Serves: 2

Ingredients To Use:
- ½ tsp of apple vinegar
- 1 smoked duck breast, cut into halves
- 1 tsp of tomato paste
- 1 tsp of honey
- 1 Tbsp of mustard

Step-by-Step Directions to Cook It:
1. Place the cooking pot into the Ninja Foodi Grill and ensure the splatter shield is in position. Close the hood.

2. Press the Bake button. Use the default temperature of 370°F and set the time for 15 minutes.
3. Press the start/stop button to preheat the appliance for 3 minutes.
4. Mix the tomato paste, honey, mustard, and vinegar in a bowl.
5. Coat the duck breasts with the honey mix and arrange them in the cooking pot.
6. Close the hood.
7. For extra taste, coat the breasts with the honey mix again and press the broil button. Use the same temperature and set the time for 6 minutes.This is only available to the Ninja Foodi Smart XL model

Serving suggestions: Serve with salad
Preparation and Cooking Tips: Flip the food halfway
Nutritional value per serving: Calories: 274kcal, Fat: 11g, Carb: 22g, Proteins: 13g

Air-Crisped Stuffed Chicken

Stuffed chickens would always be one of the best American traditions. With the Ninja Foodi Smart XL, you would be able to cook this chicken whole.
Preparation time: 10 minutes
Cooking time: 35 minutes
Serves: 8

Ingredients To Use:
- 1 whole chicken (small)
- 3 tsp of sesame oil
- 10 wolfberries
- 4 ginger slices
- 1 yam, cut into cubes
- 2 red chilies, sliced

- 1 tsp soy sauce
- Salt and white pepper, as desired

Step-by-Step Directions to Cook It:
1. Place the cooking pot into the Ninja Foodi Grill, then the crisper basket. Ensure the splatter shield is in position and close the hood.
2. Press the air crisp button. Set the temperature to 400°F and set the time for 20 minutes.
3. Press the start/stop button to preheat the appliance for 3 minutes.
4. Season the whole chicken with pepper, salt, soy sauce, and sesame oil.
5. Stuff the chicken with the whole berries, chilies, yam cubes, and ginger.
6. Transfer the chicken to the crisper basket.
7. Close the hood.
8. When the timer runs out, reduce the temperature to 360°F and increase the timer by 15 minutes.

Serving suggestions: Carve and serve with salad

Preparation and Cooking Tips: Follow the directions fastidiously

Nutritional value per serving: Calories: 320kcal, Fat: 17g, Carb: 22g, Proteins: 12g

Baked Chicken Breast with Tomato Sauce

Baked chicken breast is an awesome meal; it is perfect with salad and fits incredibly well in a low-calorie diet
Preparation time: 10 minutes
Cooking time: 20 minutes

Serves: 4
Ingredients To Use:
- 1 red onion, sliced
- ¼ tsp garlic powder
- 4 chicken skinless and boneless breasts
- 14 ounces of chopped canned tomatoes, chopped
- Salt and black pepper, as desired
- ¼ cup of balsamic vinegar
- ¼ cup of grated parmesan, grated
- Cooking spray

Step-by-Step Directions to Cook It:
1. Place the cooking pot into the Ninja Foodi Grill and ensure the splatter shield is in position. Close the hood.
2. Press the Bake button. Use the default temperature of 400°F and set the time for 20 minutes.
3. Press the start/stop button to preheat the appliance for 3 minutes.
4. Coat the baking pan with the cooking spray.
5. Season the chicken with pepper, salt, balsamic vinegar, tomatoes, garlic powder, and cheese.
6. Add the chicken to the baking pan and place it in the air fryer.
7. Close the hood.

Serving suggestions: Serve immediately

Preparation and Cooking Tips: Season the chicken appropriately for best taste

Nutritional value per serving: Calories: 250kcal, Fat: 12g, Carb: 19g, Proteins: 28g

Chicken Cacciatore

Chicken cacciatore is a delicious meal that can be taken with rice, macaroni or pasta.

Preparation time: 10 minutes
Cooking time: 20 minutes
Serves: 4

Ingredients To Use:
- Salt and black pepper, as desired
- ½ cup of pitted and sliced black olives
- 8 chicken drumsticks
- 1 bay leaf
- 1 yellow onion, sliced
- 28 ounces of crushed canned tomatoes, including juice
- 1 tsp of garlic powder
- 1 tsp of dried oregano

Step-by-Step Directions to Cook It:
1. Place the cooking pot into the Ninja Foodi Grill and ensure the splatter shield is in position. Close the hood.
2. Press the Bake button. Use the default temperature of 365°F and set the time for 20 minutes.
3. Press the start/stop button to preheat the appliance for 3 minutes.
4. Combine the chicken with the salt, garlic powder, pepper, onion, bay leaf, tomatoes and juice, olives, and oregano.
5. Transfer the mixture to a baking pan and insert it into the air fryer.
6. Close the hood.

Serving suggestions: Serve immediately

Preparation and Cooking Tips: Season the chicken correctly for best taste

Nutritional value per serving: Calories: 300kcal, Fat: 12g, Carb: 20g, Proteins: 24g

Citrus Chicken

A fitting recipe for an exotic outing. The lemon gives the chicken an incredible flavor and balances the meal perfectly. You just have to try this out now.

Preparation time: 10 minutes
Cooking time: 30 minutes
Serves: 6

Ingredients To Use:
- 1 whole chicken, chopped into pieces
- Salt and black pepper, as desired
- 2 lemons, juiced
- 1 Tbsp olive oil
- 2 lemons, zested and grated

Step-by-Step Directions to Cook It:
1. Place the cooking pot into the Ninja Foodi Grill, then the crisper basket. Ensure the splatter shield is in position and close the hood.
2. Press the air crisp button. Set the temperature to 350°F and set the time for 30 minutes.
3. Press the start/stop button to preheat the appliance for 3 minutes.
4. Rub the chicken pieces with salt, pepper, lemon zest, and oil.
5. Drizzle chicken pieces with lemon juice and transfer them to the crisper basket.
6. Close the hood

Serving suggestions: Serve with salad

Preparation and Cooking Tips: Flip the chicken halfway

Nutritional value per serving: Calories: 334kcal, Fat: 24g, Carb: 26g, Proteins: 20g

Cheese Crusted Chicken

Cheese crusted chicken is delicious and crunchy. It is a healthy meal and can be served as dinner or lunch.
Preparation time: 10 minutes
Cooking time: 15 minutes
Serves: 4

Ingredients To Use:
- ¼ tsp of garlic powder
- 4 slices of bacon, cooked and crushed
- 1 cup of grated parmesan cheese
- 4 skinless and boneless chicken breasts
- 1 Tbsp of water
- 1 egg, beaten
- Salt and black pepper, as desired
- ½ cup of avocado oil
- 1 cup of shredded asiago cheese

Step-by-Step Directions to Cook It:
1. Place the cooking pot into the Ninja Foodi Grill, then the crisper basket. Ensure the splatter shield is in position and close the hood.
2. Press the air crisp button. Set the temperature to 320°F and set the time for 15 minutes.
3. Press the start/stop button to preheat the appliance for 3 minutes.
4. Mix the parmesan, salt, pepper, and garlic in a bowl.

5. In a separate bowl, whisk the egg with water.
6. Season the chicken with salt and black pepper, then dip into the egg mix, followed by the cheese mix.
7. Transfer the chicken to the crisper basket and close the hood.

Serving suggestions: Sprinkle with bacon and asiago cheese

Preparation and Cooking Tips: Flip the chicken pieces halfway

Nutritional value per serving: Calories: 400kcal, Fat: 22g, Carb: 32g, Proteins: 47g

Ninja Pepperoni Chicken

Pepperoni chicken is tasty, spicy, straightforward, and healthy.
Preparation time: 10 minutes
Cooking time: 22 minutes
Serves: 6

Ingredients To Use:
- 2 ounces of sliced pepperoni
- 14 ounces of tomato paste
- 1 Tbsp of olive oil
- 4 medium skinless and boneless chicken breasts
- 6 ounces of sliced mozzarella
- Salt and black pepper, as desired
- 1 tsp of dried oregano
- 1 tsp of garlic powder

Step-by-Step Directions to Cook It:
1. Place the cooking pot into the Ninja Foodi Grill and ensure the splatter shield is in position. Close the hood.
2. Press the Roast button. Set the temperature to 350°F and adjust the time to 6 minutes.

3. Press the start/stop button to preheat the appliance for 3 minutes.
4. Season the chicken with salt, black pepper, oregano, and garlic powder.
5. Transfer the chicken pieces to the cooking pot and close the hood.
6. When the time is done, top the chicken pieces with the pepperoni slices and increase the timer by 15 minutes.

Serving suggestions: serve with salad
Preparation and Cooking Tips: Flip chicken pieces halfway
Nutritional value per serving: Calories: 320kcal, Fat: 10g, Carb: 23g, Proteins: 27g

Garlic Chicken

Garlic chicken has an awesome taste; it is nutritious and satisfies cravins for fried foods.
Preparation time: 10 minutes
Cooking time: 20 minutes
Serves: 4
Ingredients To Use:
- 1 Tbsp of melted butter
- ¼ cup of dry white wine
- 4 chicken breasts
- 1 Tbsp of olive oil
- 40 garlic cloves, chopped
- 2 thyme springs
- Salt and black pepper, as desired
- ¼ cup of chicken stock
- 2 Tbsp of chopped parsley

Step-by-Step Directions to Cook It:
1. Place the cooking pot into the Ninja Foodi Grill and ensure the splatter shield is in position. Close the hood.
2. Press the Bake button. Use the default temperature of 360°F and set the time for 8 minutes.
3. Press the start/stop button to preheat the appliance for 3 minutes.
4. Season the chicken with salt, pepper, and oil.
5. Transfer the chicken pieces to the cooking pot and close the hood
6. Add the melted butter, thyme, garlic, wine, stock, and parsley.
7. Increase the timer by 15 minutes and close the hood.

Serving suggestions: Serve with Salad
Preparation and Cooking Tips: Flip the chicken pieces halfway
Nutritional value per serving: Calories: 227kcal, Fat: 9g, Carb: 22g, Proteins: 12g

Duck and Veggies

This is an exceptional meal that requires no special expertise. Just get your Ninja Foodi Grill and start cooking
Preparation time: 10 minutes
Cooking time: 20 minutes
Serves: 8
Ingredients To Use:
- 1 whole duck, chopped into pieces
- 1 small ginger piece, minced
- 3 cucumbers, sliced
- 2 carrots, diced
- 3 Tbsp of white wine
- 1 cup of chicken stock
- Salt and black pepper, as desired

Step-by-Step Directions to Cook It:
1.   Place the cooking pot into the Ninja Foodi Grill. Ensure the splatter shield is in position and close the hood.
2.   Press the Bake button. Set the temperature to 370°F and set the time for 20 minutes.
3.   Press the start/stop button to preheat the appliance for 3 minutes.
4.   Combine the duck pieces, cucumbers, carrots, ginger, stock, pepper, salt, and wine in a bowl.
5.   Transfer the mixture to the cooking pot and close the hood.
Serving suggestions: serve with salad
Preparation and Cooking Tips: Flip the duck pieces halfway
Nutritional value per serving: Calories: 200kcal, Fat: 10g, Carb: 20g, Proteins: 2g

Greek Ninja Chicken

Like all great Ninja Foodi Grill recipes, this meal was tailored to satisfy your cravings and desires
Preparation time: 10 minutes
Cooking time: 15 minutes
Serves: 4
Ingredients To Use:
*   2 Tbsp of olive oil
*   1 lemon, juiced
*   1 lemon, sliced
*   1 tsp of dried oregano
*   1 zucchini,Goughly chopped
*   3 garlic cloves, grated
*   Salt and black pepper, as desired
*   1 pound of chicken drumsticks
*   ½ pound of trimmed asparagus

Step-by-Step Directions to Cook It:
1.   Place the cooking pot into the Ninja Foodi Grill, then the crisper basket. Ensure the splatter shield is in position and close the hood.
2.   Press the air crisp button. Set the temperature to 380°F and set the time for 15 minutes.
3.   Press the start/stop button to preheat the appliance for 3 minutes.
4.   Season the chicken with the oil, salt, garlic, pepper, and oregano.
5.   Transfer the seasoned chicken to the crisper basket. Drizzle with lemon juice and top with lemon slices.
6.   Add the zucchini and asparagus to the crisper basket.
7.   Close the hood.
Serving suggestions: Serve with Salad
Preparation and Cooking Tips: Flip the chicken pieces halfway
Nutritional value per serving: Calories: 300kcal, Fat: 8g, Carb: 20g, Proteins: 18g

Ninja Passion Drumsticks

Passion drumsticks are delicious; it involves a fantastic blend of passion fruit and chicken.
Preparation time: 10 minutes
Cooking time: 10 minutes
Serves: 4
Ingredients To Use:
*   4 chicken breasts
*   2 star anise
*   Salt and black pepper, as desired
*   4 passion fruits, peeled, pitted and pulp reserved
*   1 Tbsp of whiskey

- 1 bunch chives, sliced
- 2 ounces of maple syrup

Step-by-Step Directions to Cook It:

1.   Place the cooking pot into the Ninja Foodi Grill, and position the grill plate with the handles facing up.
2.   Ensure the splatter shield is in position. Close the hood.
3.   Press the Grill button. Set the temperature to 360°F and adjust the time to 10 minutes.
4.   Press the start/stop button to preheat the appliance for 8 minutes.
5.   Mix the passion fruit pulp, whiskey, star anise, chives, and maple syrup in a bowl. This will serve as the rub.
6.   Thoroughly coat the chicken pieces with the rub.
7.   Transfer to the grill plate and close the hood.

Serving suggestions: Heat the rub and serve it with the chicken

Preparation and Cooking Tips: Flip the chicken pieces halfway

Nutritional value per serving: Calories: 374kcal, Fat: 8g, Carb: 34g, Proteins: 37g

Chapter 9: Fish and Seafood Recipes

Foodi Air-Crisped Catfish

Air-Crisped catfish is a mouth-watering meal. It provides the body with vital nutrients.

Preparation time: 10 minutes
Cooking time: 20 minutes
Serves: 4

Ingredients To Use:
- 4 catfish fillets
- 1 Tbsp of olive oil
- Salt and black pepper, as desired
- 1 Tbsp of lemon juice
- Sweet paprika, a pinch
- 1 Tbsp of chopped parsley

Step-by-Step Directions to Cook It:
1. Place the cooking pot into the Ninja Foodi Grill, then the crisper basket. Ensure the splatter shield is in position and close the hood.
2. Press the air crisp button. Set the temperature to 400°F and set the time for 20 minutes.
3. Press the start/stop button to preheat the appliance for 3 minutes.
4. Season the catfish with pepper, salt, paprika, and oil.
5. Transfer to the crisper basket and close the hood.

Serving suggestions: Drizzle Lemon over catfish and sprinkle with parsley

Preparation and Cooking Tips: Flip the catfish halfway

Nutritional value per serving: Calories: 253kcal, Fat: 6g, Carb: 26g, Proteins: 22g

Ninja Baked Salmon

Baked salmon is a tasty meal and can be enjoyed as lunch or dinner.

Preparation time: 60 minutes
Cooking time: 15 minutes
Serves: 2

Ingredients To Use:
- 3 tsp of mirin
- 2 salmon fillets
- 6 Tbsp honey
- 6 Tbsp of soy sauce
- 1 tsp water

Step-by-Step Directions to Cook It:
1. Place the cooking pot into the Ninja Foodi Grill and ensure the splatter shield is in position. Close the hood.
2. Press the Bake button. Set the temperature to 360°F and adjust the time to 15 minutes.
3. Press the start/stop button to preheat the appliance for 3 minutes.
4. Mix the soy sauce, honey, mirin, salmon, and water in a bowl.
5. Keep in the fridge to marinate for an hour.
6. Transfer the salmon and marinade to the cooking pot and close the hood.

Serving suggestions: Drizzle with the marinade

Preparation and Cooking Tips: Flip the salmon after 7 minutes in the air fryer.

Nutritional value per serving: Calories: 300kcal, Fat: 12g, Carb: 13g, Proteins: 24g

Citrus Saba Fish

Citrus Saba fish is a delightful delicacy. The lemon balances the flavor and draws out the natural taste of the fish

Preparation time: 10 minutes

Cooking time: 8 minutes

Serves: 1

Ingredients To Use:

- 4 boneless Saba fish fillets
- 2 Tbsp garlic, grated
- Salt and black pepper, as desired
- 2 Tbsp of lemon juice
- 3 red chili pepper, sliced
- 2 Tbsp of olive oil

Step-by-Step Directions to Cook It:

1. Place the cooking pot into the Ninja Foodi Grill, then the crisper basket. Ensure the splatter shield is in position and close the hood.
2. Press the air crisp button. Set the temperature to 360°F and set the time for 8 minutes.
3. Press the start/stop button to preheat the appliance for 3 minutes.
4. Season the fish fillets with pepper and salt.
5. Coat the fish with lemon juice, chili, and oil
6. Transfer the seasoned fish to the crisper basket and close the hood

Serving suggestions: Serve with fries

Preparation and Cooking Tips: Flip the fish halfway

Nutritional value per serving: Calories: 300kcal, Fat: 4g, Carb: 15g, Proteins: 15g

Crab and Shrimp Meal

Crab and shrimp meal is a very nutritious meal, it can be enjoyed as dinner. It is fun to eat.

Preparation time: 10 minutes

Cooking time: 25 minutes

Serves: 4

Ingredients To Use:

- ½ cup of chopped yellow onion
- 1 tsp of sweet paprika
- 1 cup green bell pepper, sliced
- 1 cup of chopped celery
- 1 Tbsp of melted butter
- 1 pound of peeled and deveined shrimps
- 2 Tbsp of breadcrumbs
- 1 cup of flaked crabmeat
- 1 cup of mayonnaise
- Salt and black pepper, as desired
- 1 tsp of Worcestershire sauce

Step-by-Step Directions to Cook It:

1. Place the cooking pot into the Ninja Foodi Grill and ensure the splatter shield is in position. Close the hood.
2. Press the Bake button. Set the temperature to 300°F and adjust the time to 20 minutes.
3. Press the start/stop button to preheat the appliance for 3 minutes.

4.   Mix the shrimp, crab meat, onion, mayonnaise, salt, celery, pepper, Worcestershire sauce, and bell pepper in a bowl.

5.   Transfer the contents of the bowl to the cooking pot.

6.   Sprinkle the paprika, melted butter, and bread crumbs over the shrimp mix.

7.   Close the hood.

Serving suggestions: Serve immediately

Preparation and Cooking Tips: Shake halfway

Nutritional value per serving: Calories: 200kcal, Fat: 13g, Carb: 17g, Proteins: 19g

Citrus Trout Fillet

Citrus trout fillet is an elegant and delicious meal, it can be served as lunch or dinner.

Preparation time: 10 minutes
Cooking time: 10 minutes
Serves: 4

Ingredients To Use:

• 4 skinless and boneless trout fillets
• 1 orange, juiced and zested
• 4 spring onions, sliced
• 1 Tbsp ginger, grated
• 1 Tbsp of olive oil
• Salt and black pepper, as desired

Step-by-Step Directions to Cook It:

1.   Place the cooking pot into the Ninja Foodi Grill, then the crisper basket. Ensure the splatter shield is in position and close the hood.

2.   Press the air crisp button. Set the temperature to 360°F and set the time for 10 minutes.

3.   Press the start/stop button to preheat the appliance for 3 minutes.

4.   Season the fillets with pepper, salt, olive oil, ginger, and orange zest.

5.   Drizzle the trout with the orange juice and transfer it to the crisper basket.

6.   Add the green onions to the crisper basket and close the hood.

Serving suggestions: Serve immediately

Preparation and Cooking Tips: Flip trout halfway

Nutritional value per serving: Calories: 239kcal, Fat: 10g, Carb: 18g, Proteins: 23g

Trout and Butter Sauce

Trout and butter sauce is tasty. It provides your body with vital nutrients.

Preparation time: 10 minutes
Cooking time: 10 minutes
Serves: 4

Ingredients To Use:

• 4 boneless trout fillets
• Salt and black pepper, as desired
• 3 tsp of grated lemon zest
• 3 Tbsp of chopped chives
• 6 Tbsp of butter
• 2 Tbsp of olive oil
• 2 tsp of lemon juice

Step-by-Step Directions to Cook It:

1.   Place the cooking pot into the Ninja Foodi Grill, then the crisper basket. Ensure the splatter shield is in position and close the hood.

2. Press the air crisp button. Set the temperature to 360°F and set the time for 10 minutes.
3. Press the start/stop button to preheat the appliance for 3 minutes.
4. Season the trout with pepper and salt. Rub with oil.
5. Transfer to the crisper basket.
6. Remove the crisper basket and transfer the fish to the cooking pot.
7. Add the lemon juice, zest, pepper, salt, and chives to the fish and close the hood.
8. Press the broil button and set the timer for 3 minutes. This option is only available for the Ninja Foodi Smart XL.

Serving suggestions: Drizzle the butter sauce over the trout

Preparation and Cooking Tips: Flip the trout halfway

Nutritional value per serving: Calories: 300kcal, Fat: 12g, Carb: 27g, Proteins: 24g

Salmon and Avocado Salsa

Salmon and avocado salsa is a very nutritious meal, it is tasty and can be enjoyed as lunch or dinner.
Preparation time: 30 minutes
Cooking time: 10 minutes
Serves: 4

Ingredients To Use:
- 4 salmon fillets
- 1 tsp of garlic powder
- 1 Tbsp of olive oil
- 1 tsp of ground cumin
- ½ tsp of chili powder
- 1 tsp of sweet paprika

- Salt and black pepper, as desired

For the salsa:
- 1 small red onion, sliced
- Salt and black pepper, as desired
- 1 avocado, pitted, peeled, and sliced
- 2 limes, juiced
- 2 Tbsp of chopped cilantro

Step-by-Step Directions to Cook It:
1. Place the cooking pot into the Ninja Foodi Grill and ensure the splatter shield is in position. Close the hood.
2. Press the Bake button. Set the temperature to 350°F and adjust the time to 5 minutes.
3. Press the start/stop button to preheat the appliance for 3 minutes.
4. Mix the paprika, cumin, onion powder, chili powder, salt, and pepper.
5. Rub the oil and paprika mix on the salmon.
6. Transfer to the cooking pot and top with the avocado, red onion, salt, pepper, cilantro, and lime juice.
7. Close the hood.

Serving suggestions: Serve with avocado salsa

Preparation and Cooking Tips: Flip the salmon halfway

Nutritional value per serving: Calories: 300kcal, Fat: 14g, Carb: 18g, Proteins: 16g

Squid and Guacamole

Squid and guacamole is an amazing meal, it is tasty and healthy.
Preparation time: 10 minutes
Cooking time: 6 minutes
Serves: 2

Ingredients To Use:
• 2 medium squids, tentacles removed and tubes cut lengthwise
• 1 lime, juiced
• 1 Tbsp of olive oil
• Salt and black pepper, as desired
For the guacamole:
• 1 Tbsp of chopped coriander
• 2 avocados, pitted, skinned, and sliced
• 2 red chilies, sliced
• 1 red onion, sliced
• 1 tomato, sliced
• 2 limes, juiced

Step-by-Step Directions to Cook It:
1. Place the cooking pot into the Ninja Foodi Grill, then the crisper basket. Ensure the splatter shield is in position and close the hood.
2. Press the air crisp button. Set the temperature to 370°F and set the time for 30 minutes.
3. Press the start/stop button to preheat the appliance for 3 minutes.
4. Season the squid and tentacles with pepper, salt, and olive oil. Set aside.
5. Transfer the squid to the crisper basket and close the hood.
6. Mash the avocado with a fork and mix with the coriander, tomato, chilies, onion, tomato, and lime juice to make the guacamole

Serving suggestions: Top the squids with guacamole

Preparation and Cooking Tips: Shake the crisper basket halfway
Nutritional value per serving: Calories: 500kcal, Fat: 43g, Carb: 7g, Proteins: 20g

Mustard Salmon

Mustard salmon is delicious and healthy. It can be served as lunch or dinner.
Preparation time: 10 minutes
Cooking time: 10 minutes
Serves: 1

Ingredients To Use:
• 1 big salmon fillet, boneless
• 1 Tbsp of maple extract
• Salt and black pepper, as desired
• 1 Tbsp of coconut oil
• 2 Tbsp mustard

Step-by-Step Directions to Cook It:
1. Place the cooking pot into the Ninja Foodi Grill and ensure the splatter shield is in position. Close the hood.
2. Press the Bake button. Set the temperature to 370°F and adjust the time to 10 minutes.
3. Press the start/stop button to preheat the appliance for 3 minutes.
4. Mix the maple extract, mustard, salt, pepper, and salmon in a bowl.
5. Transfer the coated salmon to the cooking pot and close the hood.

Serving suggestions: Serve with a tasty salad
Preparation and Cooking Tips: Coat the salmon with cooking spray before transferring to the air fryer

Nutritional value per serving: Calories: 300kcal, Fat: 7g, Carb: 16g, Proteins: 20g

Swordfish and Special Salsa

Swordfish and special salsa is an elegant meal; it is enjoyable and healthy.

Preparation time: 10 minutes
Cooking time: 6 minutes
Serves: 2

Ingredients To Use:
- 2 medium swordfish steaks
- ½ Tbsp of balsamic vinegar
- Salt and black pepper, as desired
- 1 orange, zested and sliced
- garlic powder, a pinch
- 2 tsp of avocado oil
- onion powder, a pinch
- 1 Tbsp of chopped cilantro
- 1 mango, diced
- Cumin, a pinch
- 1 avocado, pitted, skinned, and sliced

Step-by-Step Directions to Cook It:
1. Place the cooking pot into the Ninja Foodi Grill, then the crisper basket. Ensure the splatter shield is in position and close the hood.
2. Press the air crisp button. Set the temperature to 360°F and set the time for 6 minutes.
3. Press the start/stop button to preheat the appliance for 3 minutes.
4. Season the fish with garlic powder, salt, pepper, onion powder, oil, and cumin.
5. Transfer the fish to the crisper basket and close the hood.

6. Mix the avocado, mango, vinegar, cilantro, salt, pepper, and leftover oil in a bowl to make the mango salsa

Serving suggestions: Drizzle the swordfish with the mango salsa and top with orange slices

Preparation and Cooking Tips: Flip halfway

Nutritional value per serving: Calories: 200kcal, Fat: 7g, Carb: 14g, Proteins: 14g

Foodi Air-Crisped Salmon

Air-Crisped salmon is a healthy meal. It is best enjoyed as lunch or dinner.

Preparation time: 10 minutes
Cooking time: 10 minutes
Serves: 4

Ingredients To Use:
- 1 cup of chopped pistachios
- 1 Tbsp of mustard
- 4 salmon fillets
- ¼ cup of lemon juice
- 1 tsp of chopped dill
- 2 Tbsp of honey
- Salt and black pepper, as desired

Step-by-Step Directions to Cook It:
1. Place the cooking pot into the Ninja Foodi Grill, then the crisper basket. Ensure the splatter shield is in position and close the hood.
2. Press the air crisp button. Set the temperature to 350°F and set the time for 3\10 minutes.
3. Press the start/stop button to preheat the appliance for 3 minutes.

4. Mix the pistachios, mustard, lemon juice, honey, pepper, salt, and dill in a bowl.

5. Spread the honey mix over the salmon and transfer it to the crisper basket.

6. Close the hood.

Serving suggestions: Serve with salad

Preparation and Cooking Tips: Flip the salmon halfway

Nutritional value per serving: Calories: 300kcal, Fat: 17g, Carb: 12g, Proteins: 22g

Salmon and Chives Vinaigrette

Salmon and chives vinaigrette is a delicious and healthy meal. It can be served as lunch or dinner.

Preparation time: 10 minutes
Cooking time: 12 minutes
Serves: 4

Ingredients To Use:
- 3 Tbsp of balsamic vinegar
- 2 Tbsp of chopped dill
- Salt and black pepper, as desired
- 4 boneless salmon fillets, boneless
- 1/3 cup of maple syrup
- 2 Tbsp of chopped chives
- 1 Tbsp of olive oil

Step-by-Step Directions to Cook It:
1. Place the cooking pot into the Ninja Foodi Grill and ensure the splatter shield is in position. Close the hood.

2. Press the Bake button. Set the temperature to 350°F and adjust the time to 8minutes.

3. Press the start/stop button to preheat the appliance for 3 minutes.

4. Season the fish with salt, pepper, and oil.

5. Transfer to the cooking pot and close the hood.

6. Add the vinegar, maple syrup, chives, and dill.

7. Increase the timer by 3 minutes.

Serving suggestions: Top with chives vinaigrette

Preparation and Cooking Tips: Flip salmon halfway

Nutritional value per serving: Calories: 270kcal, Fat: 3g, Carb: 25g, Proteins: 10g

Foodi Roasted Cod and Prosciutto

Roasted cod and prosciutto is a delicious meal. It is fun to eat and healthy.

Preparation time: 10 minutes
Cooking time: 10 minutes
Serves: 4

Ingredients To Use:
- 1 shallot, grated
- 1 Tbsp of chopped parsley
- Salt and black pepper, as desired
- 4 medium cod fillets
- 1 tsp of Dijon mustard
- ¼ cup of melted butter
- 2 garlic cloves, grated
- 3 Tbsp of chopped prosciutto, chopped
- 2 Tbsp of lemon juice

Step-by-Step Directions to Cook It:
1. Place the cooking pot into the Ninja Foodi Grill, then the crisper

basket. Ensure the splatter shield is in position and close the hood.

2. Press the air crisp button. Set the temperature to 390°F and set the time for 10 minutes.

3. Press the start/stop button to preheat the appliance for 3 minutes.

4. Mix the mustard, butter, garlic, parsley, lemon juice, shallot, salt, black pepper, and prosciutto in a bowl.

5. Rub the fish with salt and pepper, then coat with the prosciutto mix.

6. Transfer the coated fish to the air fryer and close the hood

Serving suggestions: Serve immediately

Preparation and Cooking Tips: Flip halfway

Nutritional value per serving: Calories: 200kcal, Fat: 4g, Carb: 12g, Proteins: 6g

Ninja Halibut Tomatoes Meal

Halibut tomato meal is a great choice for dinner; it is mouth-watering and healthy.

Preparation time: 10 minutes
Cooking time: 10 minutes
Serves: 2

Ingredients To Use:
- 2 garlic cloves, grated
- 2 medium halibut fillets
- 2 tsp of olive oil
- 9 black olives, deseeded and chopped
- 2 small red onions, chopped
- 6 sun dried tomatoes, sliced
- 1 fennel bulb, chopped

- 4 chopped rosemary springs
- Salt and black pepper, as desired
- ½ tsp of crushed red pepper flakes

Step-by-Step Directions to Cook It:

1. Place the cooking pot into the Ninja Foodi Grill and ensure the splatter shield is in position. Close the hood.

2. Press the Roast button. Set the temperature to 380°F and adjust the time to 10 minutes.

3. Press the start/stop button to preheat the appliance for 3 minutes.

4. Season the fish with pepper, salt, oil, and garlic.

5. Transfer the fish to the air fryer and add the onion slices, tomatoes, olives, fennel, rosemary, and pepper flakes.

6. Close the hood.

Serving suggestions: Serve immediately with the veggies

Preparation and Cooking Tips: Flip halfway

Nutritional value per serving: Calories: 300kcal, Fat: 12g, Carb: 18g, Proteins: 30g

Foodi Flavored Salmon

Flavoured salmon is tasty, and healthy. It can be served as dinner or lunch.

Preparation time: 60 minutes
Cooking time: 8 minutes
Serves: 2

Ingredients To Use:
- 1/3 cup of brown sugar
- 2 Tbsp of lemon juice

- 2 salmon fillets
- Salt and black pepper, as desired
- 1/3 cup of water
- ½ tsp of garlic powder
- 1/3 cup of soy sauce
- 3 scallions, sliced
- 2 Tbsp of olive oil

Step-by-Step Directions to Cook It:

1. Place the cooking pot into the Ninja Foodi Grill and ensure the splatter shield is in position. Close the hood.
2. Press the Bake button. Set the temperature to 360°F and adjust the time to 8 minutes.
3. Press the start/stop button to preheat the appliance for 3 minutes.
4. Mix the water, sugar, garlic powder, soy sauce, salt, oil, black pepper, and lemon juice in a bowl.
5. Coat the salmon with the lemon mix and marinate in the fridge for one hour.
6. Transfer the flavored salmon to the air fryer and close the hood.

Serving suggestions: Sprinkle with scallions and serve immediately

Preparation and Cooking Tips: Flip salmon halfway

Nutritional value per serving: Calories: 300kcal, Fat: 12g, Carb: 23g, Proteins: 20g

Chapter 10: Bread, Bagel, and Pizza Recipes

Cheese Bread

Cheese bread is an elegant and delicious meal. It's best served as dinner. It provides the body with vital nutrients.

Preparation time: 10 minutes
Cooking time: 8 minutes
Serves: 3

Ingredients To Use:
- 5 Tbsp of melted butter
- 6 bread slices
- 1 cup of grated mozzarella cheese
- 3 garlic cloves, grated
- 6 tsp of sun-dried tomato pesto

Step-by-Step Directions to Cook It:
1. Place the cooking pot into the Ninja Foodi Grill and ensure the splatter shield is in position. Close the hood.
2. Press the Bake button. Set the temperature to 350°F and adjust the time to 8 minutes.
3. Press the start/stop button to preheat the appliance for 3 minutes.
4. Arrange the bread slices on a flat surface and butter them.
5. Spread the tomato paste on the bread, add garlic and top with mozzarella cheese.
6. Transfer the bread slices to the cooking pot and close the hood.

Serving suggestions: Serve hot

Preparation and Cooking Tips: Flip the bread halfway
Nutritional value per serving: Calories: 187kcal, Fat: 5g, Carb: 8g, Proteins: 3g

Bread Pudding

Bread pudding is an amazing meal. It is a healthy meal and can be served as dinner.

Preparation time: 10 minutes
Cooking time: 22 minutes
Serves: 4

Ingredients To Use:
- ½ pound of cubed white bread
- 3 ounces of soft butter
- ¾ cup of milk
- ¾ cup of water
- 3/5 cup of brown sugar
- 2 tsp of cornstarch
- 11/3 cup of flour
- ½ cup apple, peeled, cored and roughly chopped
- 5 Tbsp of honey
- 2 tsp of cinnamon powder
- 1 tsp of vanilla extract

Step-by-Step Directions to Cook It:
1. Place the cooking pot into the Ninja Foodi Grill and ensure the splatter shield is in position. Close the hood.
2. Press the Bake button. Set the temperature to 350°F and adjust the time to 22 minutes.

3.   Press the start/stop button to preheat the appliance for 3 minutes.
4.   Mix the bread, apple, milk, water, honey, vanilla, cinnamon, and cornstarch in a bowl
5.   In another bowl, mix the flour, butter, and sugar thoroughly to obtain a crumbled mixture.
6.   Spread half of the butter mix on the cooking pot.
7.   Add the bread and apple mix.
8.   Top with the rest of the butter mix.
9.   Close the hood.

Serving suggestions: Serve with Orange juice

Preparation and Cooking Tips: Stir the butter mix thoroughly.

Nutritional value per serving: Calories: 262kcal, Fat: 7g, Carb: 8g, Proteins: 5g

Foodi Bread Rolls

Bread rolls are delightful. Nothing beats the flavor and aroma of freshly baked bread. This is one of the many amazing delicacies possible with the Ninja Foodi Grill

Preparation time: 10 minutes
Cooking time: 12 minutes
Serves: 4

Ingredients To Use:
- ½ tsp of turmeric powder
- 5 boiled potatoes, skinned and mashed
- Salt and black pepper, as desired
- 8 bread slices, edges cut off
- 2 Tbsp of olive oil
- 1 coriander bunch, slice
- ½ tsp of mustard seeds
- 2 green chilies, sliced
- 2 curry leaf springs
- 2 small yellow onions, sliced

Step-by-Step Directions to Cook It:
1.   Place the cooking pot into the Ninja Foodi Grill and ensure the splatter shield is in position. Close the hood.
2.   Press the Bake button. Set the temperature to 300°F and adjust the time to 2 minutes.
3.   Press the start/stop button to preheat the appliance for 3 minutes.
4.   Add 1 tsp of olive oil to the cooking pot, add the onion, mustard, turmeric, and curry leaves.
5.   Add the coriander, salt, pepper, chilies, and mashed potatoes, and close the hood.
6.   Remove the potato mix from the appliance and set aside.
7.   Divide the potatoes mixture into 8 parts and shape into ovals with wet hands.
8.   Wet the bread with water, drain excess moisture, and spread it over your palm. Add 1 of the potato ovals to the bread and wrap it with the bread.
9.   Repeat step 9 for the other bread slices and potato ovals.
10.   Grease the cooking pot with the rest of the oil and add the bread rolls
11.   Increase the temperature to 400°F and set the timer for 12 minutes.

Serving suggestions: Serve Hot
Preparation and Cooking Tips: Follow the instructions fastidiously

Nutritional value per serving: Calories: 261kcal, Fat: 6g, Carb: 12g, Proteins: 7g

Raspberry Rolls

Raspberry rolls are tasty and have an incredible aroma. Try this recipe out now with your Ninja Foodi Grill
Preparation time: 30 minutes
Cooking time: 20 minutes
Serves: 6

Ingredients To Use:
- 2 tsp of yeast
- 1 cup of milk
- 1 egg
- 4 Tbsp of butter
- ¼ cup sugar
- 3¼ cups of flour

For the filling:
- 5 Tbsp of sugar
- 8 ounces of soft cream cheese
- 1 lemon, zested and grated
- 12 ounces of raspberries
- 1 Tbsp of cornstarch
- 1 tsp of vanilla extract

Step-by-Step Directions to Cook It:
1.   Place the cooking pot into the Ninja Foodi Grill and ensure the splatter shield is in position. Close the hood.
2.   Press the Bake button. Set the temperature to 350°F and adjust the time to 30 minutes.
3.   Press the start/stop button to preheat the appliance for 3 minutes.
4.   Mix the flour, sugar, and yeast in a bowl.
5.   Add the egg and milk. Stir until a dough is obtained.

6.   Set aside the dough for 30 minutes to allow rising.
7.   Spread dough on a flat surface and roll.
8.   Mix the cheese, sugar, lemon zest, and vanilla in a bowl. Spread over the dough.
9.   Mix the raspberry and cornstarch in another bowl and spread over the cheese mix. Roll the dough again and cut into medium sizes.
10.   Transfer them to the cooking pot and spray with cooking spray.
11.   Close the hood.

Serving suggestions: Serve Hot
Preparation and Cooking Tips: Follow the recipe recommendations fastidiously
Nutritional value per serving: Calories: 261kcal, Fat: 5g, Carb: 9g, Proteins: 6g

Ham Rolls

Ham rolls are delicious and fun to eat. They nourish the body.
Preparation time: 10 minutes
Cooking time: 10 minutes
Serves: 4

Ingredients To Use:
- 8 ham slices, sliced
- 1 sheet puff pastry
- 4 tsp of mustard
- 4 handful of grated gruyere cheese, grated

Step-by-Step Directions to Cook It:
1.   Place the cooking pot into the Ninja Foodi Grill and ensure the

splatter shield is in position. Close the hood.

2.   Press the Bake button. Set the temperature to 370°F and adjust the time to 10 minutes.

3.   Press the start/stop button to preheat the appliance for 3 minutes.

4.   Roll out the pastry on a flat surface.

5.   Add cheese, mustard, and ham to the puff pastry.

6.   Roll tight and cut the pastry into medium rolls.

7.   Transfer the rolls to the cooking pot and close the hood.

Serving suggestions: Serve Hot

Preparation and Cooking Tips: Roll the puff pastry well

Nutritional value per serving: Calories: 182kcal, Fat: 4g, Carb: 9g, Proteins: 8g

Quick Foodi Pizza

Quick pizza is an awesome choice for dinner. It is fun to eat.

Preparation time: 10 minutes

Cooking time: 7 minutes

Serves: 4

Ingredients To Use:

- 4 ounces of jarred mushrooms, chopped
- 4 pitas
- 1 Tbsp of olive oil
- 1 cup of sliced grape tomatoes
- ¾ cup of pizza sauce
- ½ tsp of dried basil
- 2 cups of grated mozzarella
- 2 green onions, sliced

Step-by-Step Directions to Cook It:

1.   Place the cooking pot into the Ninja Foodi Grill and ensure the splatter shield is in position. Close the hood.

2.   Press the Bake button. Set the temperature to 400°F and adjust the time to 7 minutes.

3.   Press the start/stop button to preheat the appliance for 3 minutes.

4.   Spread the pizza sauce on each bread and top with green onion and basil.

5.   Add the chopped mushroom to the pizza and top with cheese.

6.   Transfer the pizza to the cooking pot and close the hood.

Serving suggestions: Top the pizza with slices of tomato and divide.

Preparation and Cooking Tips: Ensure the pizza sauce is spread consistently

Nutritional value per serving: Calories: 200kcal, Fat: 4g, Carb: 7g, Proteins: 3g

Prosciutto Sandwich

Prosciutto sandwich is a tasty meal. It's an amazing idea for dinner.

Preparation time: 10 minutes

Cooking time: 5 minutes

Serves: 1

Ingredients To Use:

- salt and black pepper, a pinch
- 2 bread slices
- 2 prosciutto slices
- 2 mozzarella slices
- 2 basil leaves
- 2 tomato slices
- 1 tsp of olive oil

Step-by-Step Directions to Cook It:

1. Place the cooking pot into the Ninja Foodi Grill and ensure the splatter shield is in position. Close the hood.
2. Press the Bake button. Set the temperature to 400°F and adjust the time to 5 minutes.
3. Press the start/stop button to preheat the appliance for 3 minutes.
4. Spread the bread slices on a flat surface and top with mozzarella cheese and prosciutto.
5. Season with salt and black pepper.
6. Transfer to the air fryer and close the hood.
7. Add tomato and basil.
8. Drizzle oil over the prosciutto and cover with the other slice.

Serving suggestions: Halve sandwich and serve

Preparation and Cooking Tips: Follow the instructions fastidiously

Nutritional value per serving: Calories: 171kcal, Fat: 3g, Carb: 9g, Proteins: 5g

Cheese Ravioli Meal

Cheese ravioli meal is tasty and nutritious, best served as dinner.
Preparation time: 10 minutes
Cooking time: 8 minutes
Serves: 6

Ingredients To Use:
- 20 ounces of cheese ravioli
- ¼ cup of grated parmesan
- 10 ounces of marinara sauce
- 1 Tbsp of olive oil
- 2 cups of bread crumbs
- 1 cup of buttermilk

Step-by-Step Directions to Cook It:
1. Place the cooking pot into the Ninja Foodi Grill and ensure the splatter shield is in position. Close the hood.
2. Press the Bake button. Set the temperature to 400°F and adjust the time to 5 minutes.
3. Press the start/stop button to preheat the appliance for 3 minutes.
4. Put the buttermilk and breadcrumbs in a separate bowl.
5. Dip the cheese ravioli in the buttermilk, followed by the breadcrumbs.
6. Line the cooking pot with a baking sheet and arrange the cheese ravioli on the baking sheet.
7. Close the hood.

Serving suggestions: Serve immediately

Preparation and Cooking Tips: Drizzle the ravioli with olive oil before cooking

Nutritional value per serving: Calories: 270kcal, Fat: 12g, Carb: 30g, Proteins: 15g

Crispy Brussels and Potatoes

Crispy Brussels and potatoes are delightful. It's Got an awesome taste and provides the body with nutrients.
Preparation time: 10 minutes
Cooking time: 8 minutes
Serves: 4

Ingredients To Use:
- Salt and black pepper, as desired
- 1½ pounds of Brussels sprouts, trimmed

- 1½ Tbsp of butter
- 1½ Tbsp of bread crumbs
- 1 cup of chopped new potatoes

Step-by-Step Directions to Cook It:
1. Place the cooking pot into the Ninja Foodi Grill, then the crisper basket. Ensure the splatter shield is in position and close the hood.
2. Press the air crisp button. Set the temperature to 400°F and set the time for 8 minutes.
3. Press the start/stop button to preheat the appliance for 3 minutes.
4. Transfer the Brussel sprout and potatoes to the crisper basket.
5. Add the breadcrumbs, pepper, salt, and butter.
6. Close the hood.

Serving suggestions: Serve as a side dish

Preparation and Cooking Tips: Shake the basket halfway

Nutritional value per serving: Calories: 152kcal, Fat: 3g, Carb: 17g, Proteins: 4g

Coconut and Chicken Bites

Coconut and chicken bites are delicious and healthy.
Preparation time: 10 minutes
Cooking time: 13 minutes
Serves: 4

Ingredients To Use:
- 2 tsp of garlic powder
- 8 chicken tenders
- 2 eggs
- Cooking spray
- Salt and black pepper, as desired

- ¾ cup of shredded coconut
- ¾ cup of panko bread crumbs

Step-by-Step Directions to Cook It:
1. Place the cooking pot into the Ninja Foodi Grill, then the crisper basket. Ensure the splatter shield is in position and close the hood.
2. Press the air crisp button. Set the temperature to 350°F and set the time for 10 minutes.
3. Press the start/stop button to preheat the appliance for 3 minutes.
4. Mix the eggs, pepper, salt, and garlic powder in a bowl.
5. In a separate bowl, mix the panko and the coconut.
6. Dip the chicken into the egg mix and then the coconut mix.
7. Spray the chicken with cooking spray and transfer to the crisper basket.
8. Close the hood.

Serving suggestions: Serve as an appetizer

Preparation and Cooking Tips: Shake the crisper basket halfway

Nutritional value per serving: Calories: 252kcal, Fat: 4g, Carb: 14g, Proteins: 24g

Buffalo Cauliflower Snack

Buffalo cauliflower snack is tasty and a great idea for dinner.
Preparation time: 10 minutes
Cooking time: 15 minutes
Serves: 4

Ingredients To Use:
- 4 cups of cauliflower florets
- ¼ cup of buffalo sauce
- 1 cup of panko bread crumbs

- Mayonnaise
- ¼ cup of melted butter

Step-by-Step Directions to Cook It:
1.   Place the cooking pot into the Ninja Foodi Grill, then the crisper basket. Ensure the splatter shield is in position and close the hood.
2.   Press the air crisp button. Set the temperature to 350°F and set the time for 15 minutes.
3.   Press the start/stop button to preheat the appliance for 3 minutes.
4.   Mix the butter and buffalo sauce.
5.   Dip the cauliflower in the buffalo mix and cost them with panko bread crumbs.
6.   Transfer them to the crisper basket and close the hood.

Serving suggestions: Serve with Mayo
Preparation and Cooking Tips: Shake the crisper basket halfway
Nutritional value per serving: Calories: 241kcal, Fat: 4g, Carb: 8g, Proteins: 4g

BreadSticks

Breadsticks are delicious and are amazing to have as dinner.
Preparation time: 10minutes
Cooking time: 10 minutes
Serves: 2

Ingredients To Use:
- 4 bread slices, cut into 16 sticks
- ¼ cup of milk
- Nutmeg, a pinch
- 1 tsp of cinnamon powder
- 2 eggs
- ¼ cup of brown sugar
- 1 Tbsp of honey

Step-by-Step Directions to Cook It:
1.   Place the cooking pot into the Ninja Foodi Grill, then the crisper basket. Ensure the splatter shield is in position and close the hood.
2.   Press the air crisp button. Set the temperature to 360°F and set the time for 10 minutes.
3.   Press the start/stop button to preheat the appliance for 3 minutes.
4.   Mix the eggs, sugar, milk, nutmeg, cinnamon, and honey.
5.   Dip the breadsticks into the cinnamon mix and transfer to the crisper basket.
6.   Close the hood

Serving suggestions: Serve as a snack
Preparation and Cooking Tips: Shake the basket halfway
Nutritional value per serving: Calories: 140kcal, Fat: 1g, Carb: 8g, Proteins: 4g

Crispy Fish Sticks

Crispy fish sticks are delightful and crunchy. They are also great snacks and should be your go-to recipe when searching for a diet-friendly, tasty snack.
Preparation time: 10 minutes
Cooking time: 12 minutes
Serves: 2

Ingredients To Use:
- 4 ounces of bread crumbs
- 1 egg, beaten
- 4 Tbsp of olive oil
- Salt and black pepper, as desired

- 4 boneless, skinless white fish filets, cut into medium sticks

Step-by-Step Directions to Cook It:

1. Place the cooking pot into the Ninja Foodi Grill, then the crisper basket. Ensure the splatter shield is in position and close the hood.
2. Press the air crisp button. Set the temperature to 360°F and set the time for 12 minutes.
3. Press the start/stop button to preheat the appliance for 3 minutes.
4. Combine the bread crumbs and oil in a bowl.
5. In a separate bowl, mix the egg, salt, and pepper.
6. Dip the fish sticks in the egg mix, then in the bread crumb mix, then transfer to the crisper basket.
7. Close the hood

Serving suggestions: Serve as an appetizer

Preparation and Cooking Tips: Shake the basket halfway

Nutritional value per serving: Calories: 160kcal, Fat: 3g, Carb: 12g, Proteins: 3g

Bread Dough and Amaretto Dessert

Bread dough and amaretto dessert is a meal you will enjoy. It's nutritious.
Preparation time: 10 minutes
Cooking time: 12 minutes
Serves: 12

Ingredients To Use:
- 1 pound of bread dough
- ½ cup of melted butter
- 1 cup of sugar
- 1 cup of heavy cream
- 2 Tbsp of amaretto liqueur

- 12 ounces of chocolate chips

Step-by-Step Directions to Cook It:

1. Place the cooking pot into the Ninja Foodi Grill and ensure the splatter shield is in position. Close the hood.
2. Press the Bake button. Set the temperature to 350°F and adjust the time to 8 minutes.
3. Press the start/stop button to preheat the appliance for 3 minutes.
4. Roll the dough and cut into 20 slices.
5. Cut each slice into two.
6. Brush the dough slices with butter, sprinkle with sugar, and coat again with butter.
7. Transfer the coated dough slices to the crisper basket and close the hood.
8. Remove the dough slices and the crisper basket.
9. Add the heavy cream and chocolate chips into the cooking pot. Increase the timer by 2 minutes to melt.
10. Add the liqueur to the cream mix and stir.

Serving suggestions: Serve bread dippers with the liqueur sauce

Preparation and Cooking Tips: Flip the crisper basket after 5 minutes

Nutritional value per serving: Calories: 200kcal, Fat: 1g, Carb: 6g, Proteins: 6g

Banana Bread

Banana bread has a delightful taste, it excites the taste buds. It's nutritious.
Preparation time: 10 minutes

Cooking time: 40 minutes
Serves: 6

Ingredients To Use:

- ¾ cup of sugar
- Cooking spray
- 1/3 cup of butter
- 1½ tsp of cream of tartar
- 1 tsp of vanilla extract
- 1 egg
- 1/3 cup of milk
- ½ tsp of baking soda
- 2 bananas, mashed
- 1½ cups of flour
- 1 tsp of baking powder

Nutritional value per serving: Calories: 292kcal, Fat: 7g, Carb: 28g, Proteins: 4g

Step-by-Step Directions to Cook It:

1. Place the cooking pot into the Ninja Foodi Grill and ensure the splatter shield is in position. Close the hood.
2. Press the Bake button. Set the temperature to 320°F and adjust the time to 4 minutes.
3. Press the start/stop button to preheat the appliance for 3 minutes.
4. Mix the milk, cream of tartar, butter, egg, sugar, vanilla, and bananas in a bowl.
5. In a separate bowl, mix the flour, baking powder, and baking soda.
6. Combine both mixtures and pour into a baking pan.
7. Fit the baking pan into the air fryer and close the hood.

Serving suggestions: Cool the bread before serving

Preparation and Cooking Tips: Coat the baking pan with cooking spray before adding the two mixtures.

Chapter 11: Vegan and Vegetarian Recipes

Cheesy Artichokes

Cheesy Artichokes are amazing. They're nutritious and fun to eat.
Preparation time: 10 minutes
Cooking time: 6 minutes
Serves: 6

Ingredients To Use:
- 14 ounces of canned artichoke hearts
- 1 tsp of onion powder
- 8 ounces of cream cheese
- ½ cup of mayonnaise
- 16 ounces of grated parmesan cheese
- 3 garlic cloves, grated
- 10 ounces of spinach
- ½ cup of chicken stock
- ½ cup of sour cream
- 8 ounces of shredded mozzarella

Step-by-Step Directions to Cook It:
1. Place the cooking pot into the Ninja Foodi Grill and ensure the splatter shield is in position. Close the hood.
2. Press the Bake button. Set the temperature to 350°F and adjust the time to 6 minutes.
3. Press the start/stop button to preheat the appliance for 3 minutes.
4. Mix the artichokes, stock, garlic, cream cheese, sour cream, mayo, and onion powder in a bowl.
5. Transfer to the cooking pot and close the hood.

Serving suggestions: Top with mozzarella and parmesan cheese
Preparation and Cooking Tips: Stir before serving
Nutritional value per serving: Calories: 261kcal, Fat: 12g, Carb: 12g, Proteins: 15g

Artichokes and Anchovy sauce

Artichokes and anchovy sauce are delicious. They're great as dinner.
Preparation time: 10 minutes
Cooking time: 6 minutes
Serves: 2

Ingredients To Use:
- 2 garlic cloves, grated
- ½ tsp of olive oil
- 1 Tbsp of lemon juice
- 2 artichokes, trimmed

For the sauce:
- ¼ cup extra virgin olive oil
- 3 garlic cloves
- ¼ cup of coconut oil
- 3 anchovy fillets

Step-by-Step Directions to Cook It:
1. Place the cooking pot into the Ninja Foodi Grill and ensure the splatter shield is in position. Close the hood.
2. Press the Bake button. Set the temperature to 350°F and adjust the time to 6 minutes.

3. Press the start/stop button to preheat the appliance for 3 minutes.
4. Mix the artichokes, oil, two garlic cloves, and lemon juice in a bowl.
5. Transfer the coated artichokes to the cooking pot and close the hood
6. Blend the anchovy, coconut oil, and garlic cloves with a food processor.
Serving suggestions: Drizzle anchovy sauce over artichokes
Preparation and Cooking Tips: Flip the artichokes halfway
Nutritional value per serving: Calories: 261kcal, Fat: 4g, Carb: 20g, Proteins: 12g

Beets and Blue Cheese Salad

Beets and blue cheese salad are awesome. They're nutritious and healthy.
Preparation time: 10 minutes
Cooking time: 14 minutes
Serves: 6
Ingredients To Use:
- 6 beets, unpeeled and quartered
- Salt and black pepper, as desired
- ¼ cup of blue cheese, crumbled
- 1 Tbsp of olive oil
Step-by-Step Directions to Cook It:
1. Place the cooking pot into the Ninja Foodi Grill, then the crisper basket. Ensure the splatter shield is in position and close the hood.

2. Press the air crisp button. Set the temperature to 370°F and set the time for 30 minutes.
3. Press the start/stop button to preheat the appliance for 3 minutes.
4. Transfer the beets to the crisper basket and close the hood.
5. Mix the beets, blue cheese, salt, pepper, and oil on a plate.
Serving suggestions: Serve immediately
Preparation and Cooking Tips: Shake the basket halfway
Nutritional value per serving: Calories: 100kcal, Fat: 4g, Carb: 10g, Proteins: 5g

Broccoli Salad

Broccoli salad is fun to eat. It is delicious and provides the body with vitamins.
Preparation time: 10 minutes
Cooking time: 8 minutes
Serves: 4
Ingredients To Use:
- 6 garlic cloves, grated
- 1 broccoli head, florets separated
- 1 Tbsp of Chinese rice wine vinegar
- 1 Tsp of peanut oil
- Salt and black pepper, as desired
Step-by-Step Directions to Cook It:
1. Place the cooking pot into the Ninja Foodi Grill, then the crisper basket. Ensure the splatter shield is in position and close the hood.

2. Press the air crisp button. Set the temperature to 350°F and set the time for 8 minutes.
3. Press the start/stop button to preheat the appliance for 3 minutes.
4. Mix the broccoli, salt, pepper, and ½ of the oil in a bowl.
5. Transfer to the air fryer and close the hood.
6. Add the rest of the oil, garlic, and rice vinegar to the broccoli.
7. Toss.
Serving suggestions: Serve immediately
Preparation and Cooking Tips: Shake the basket halfway
Nutritional value per serving: Calories: 121kcal, Fat: 3g, Carb: 4g, Proteins: 4g

Baby Carrots Dish

Baby carrots are tasty and crunchy. They're nutritious and fun to eat.
Preparation time: 10 minutes
Cooking time: 10 minutes
Serves: 4
Ingredients To Use:
- 2 cups of baby carrots
- salt and black pepper, a pinch
- 1 Tbsp of brown sugar
- ½ Tbsp of melted butter

Step-by-Step Directions to Cook It:
1. Place the cooking pot into the Ninja Foodi Grill, then the crisper basket. Ensure the splatter shield is in position and close the hood.
2. Press the air crisp button. Set the temperature to 350°F and set the time for 10 minutes.

3. Press the start/stop button to preheat the appliance for 3 minutes.
4. Mix the baby carrots, butter, salt, sugar, and black pepper in a bowl.
5. Transfer the coated baby carrots to the crisper basket and close the hood.
Serving suggestions: Serve immediately
Preparation and Cooking Tips: Shake the basket halfway
Nutritional value per serving: Calories: 100kcal, Fat: 2g, Carb: 7g, Proteins: 4g

Air-Crisped Leeks

Air-crisped leeks are tasty and nutritious. Try this recipe out now on your Ninja Foodi Grill for a truly remarkable experience

Preparation time: 10 minutes
Cooking time: 7 minutes
Serves: 4
Ingredients To Use:
- 1 Tbsp of melted butter
- 4 leeks, ends cut off and cut into halves
- 1 Tbsp of lemon juice
- Salt and black pepper, as desired
Step-by-Step Directions to Cook It:
1. Place the cooking pot into the Ninja Foodi Grill, then the crisper basket. Ensure the splatter shield is in position and close the hood.
2. Press the air crisp button. Set the temperature to 350°F and set the time for 7 minutes.

3. Press the start/stop button to preheat the appliance for 3 minutes.
4. Mix the melted butter, salt, leeks, and black pepper in a bowl.
5. Transfer the coated leeks to the crisper basket and close the hood.
Serving suggestions: Drizzle with lemon juice
Preparation and Cooking Tips: Shake the basket halfway
Nutritional value per serving: Calories: 100kcal, Fat: 4g, Carb: 6g, Proteins: 2g

Air-Crisped Potatoes and Parsley

Air-crisped potatoes and parsley are crunchy and tasty. They provide the body with vital nutrients.
Preparation time: 10 minutes
Cooking time: 10 minutes
Serves: 4
Ingredients To Use:
• 2 Tbsp of olive
• ¼ cup of chopped parsley leaves
• 1 pound of potatoes, cut into medium chunks
• ½ lemon, juiced
• Salt and black pepper, as desired
Step-by-Step Directions to Cook It:
1. Place the cooking pot into the Ninja Foodi Grill, then the crisper basket. Ensure the splatter shield is in position and close the hood.
2. Press the air crisp button. Set the temperature to 350°F and set the time for 10 minutes.
3. Press the start/stop button to preheat the appliance for 3 minutes.

4. Mix the potatoes, lemon juice, olive oil, salt, and black pepper in a bowl.
5. Transfer the potatoes to the crisper basket and close the hood.
Serving suggestions: Sprinkle with parsley and serve
Preparation and Cooking Tips: Shake the basket halfway
Nutritional value per serving: Calories: 152kcal, Fat: 3g, Carb: 17g, Proteins: 4g

Radish Hash

Radish hash is crunchy and tasty. It is fun to eat and a great choice for dinner.
Preparation time: 10 minutes
Cooking time: 7 minutes
Serves: 4
Ingredients To Use:
• Salt and black pepper, as desired
• ½ tsp of onion powder
• 1/3 cups of grated parmesan
• 1 pound of radishes, chopped
• 4 eggs
• ½ tsp of garlic powder
Step-by-Step Directions to Cook It:
1. Place the cooking pot into the Ninja Foodi Grill, then the crisper basket. Ensure the splatter shield is in position and close the hood.
2. Press the air crisp button. Set the temperature to 350°F and set the time for 7 minutes.
3. Press the start/stop button to preheat the appliance for 3 minutes.

4. Mix the radishes, garlic powder, onion, salt, eggs, parmesan, and black pepper in a bowl.
5. Transfer the coated radishes to the crisper basket and close the hood.

Serving suggestions: Serve immediately

Preparation and Cooking Tips: Shake the basket halfway

Nutritional value per serving: Calories: 80kcal, Fat: 5g, Carb: 5g, Proteins: 7g

Air-Crisped Tomatoes

Air-crisped tomatoes are nutritious; they provide the body with vitamins and nutrients.

Preparation time: 10 minutes
Cooking time: 15 minutes
Serves: 8

Ingredients To Use:
- 1 jalapeno pepper, sliced
- ½ cup of grated parmesan
- 4 garlic cloves, grated
- 2 pounds of cherry tomatoes, cut into halves
- ¼ cup of chopped basil
- Salt and black pepper, as desired
- ½ tsp of dried oregano
- ¼ cup of olive oil

Step-by-Step Directions to Cook It:
1. Place the cooking pot into the Ninja Foodi Grill, then the crisper basket. Ensure the splatter shield is in position and close the hood.
2. Press the air crisp button. Set the temperature to 380°F and set the time for 15 minutes.

3. Press the start/stop button to preheat the appliance for 3 minutes.
4. Mix the tomatoes, garlic, oregano, jalapeno, oil, and black pepper in a bowl.
5. Transfer the coated tomatoes to the crisper basket and close the hood.

Serving suggestions: Sprinkle with basil and parmesan

Preparation and Cooking Tips: Shake the basket halfway

Nutritional value per serving: Calories: 140kcal, Fat: 2g, Carb: 6g, Proteins: 8g

Garlic Tomatoes

Garlic tomatoes are tasty and nutritious. It can be served as dinner and lunch.

Preparation time: 10 minutes
Cooking time: 15 minutes
Serves: 4

Ingredients To Use:
- 4 garlic cloves, grounded
- ¼ cup of olive oil
- 1 pound of mixed tomatoes
- Salt and black pepper, as desired
- 3 thyme springs, sliced

Step-by-Step Directions to Cook It:
1. Place the cooking pot into the Ninja Foodi Grill, then the crisper basket. Ensure the splatter shield is in position and close the hood.
2. Press the air crisp button. Set the temperature to 360°F and set the time for 15 minutes.
3. Press the start/stop button to preheat the appliance for 3 minutes.

4. Mix the tomatoes, olive oil, thyme, salt and black pepper in a bowl.

5. Transfer the coated tomatoes to the crisper basket and close the hood.

Serving suggestions: Serve immediately

Preparation and Cooking Tips: Shake the basket halfway

Nutritional value per serving: Calories: 100kcal, Fat: 0g, Carb: 1g, Proteins: 6g

Green Beans and Tomatoes

Green beans and tomatoes are rich in vitamins and nutrients and can be served as dinner or lunch.

Preparation time: 10 minutes
Cooking time: 15 minutes
Serves: 4

Ingredients To Use:

- Salt and black pepper, as desired
- 1 pint of cherry tomatoes
- 2 Tbsp of olive oil
- 1 pound of green beans

Step-by-Step Directions to Cook It:

1. Place the cooking pot into the Ninja Foodi Grill, then the crisper basket.

2. Ensure the splatter shield is in position and close the hood.

3. Press the air crisp button. Set the temperature to 400°F and set the time for 15 minutes.

4. Press the start/stop button to preheat the appliance for 3 minutes.

5. Mix the cherry tomatoes, beans, salt, pepper, and olive oil in a bowl.

6. Transfer to the crisper basket and close the hood.

Serving suggestions: Serve immediately

Preparation and Cooking Tips: Shake the basket halfway

Nutritional value per serving: Calories: 162kcal, Fat: 6g, Carb: 8g, Proteins: 9g

Flavored Green Beans

Flavored green beans are tasty and a great choice to have as dinner. It provides the body with necessary nutrients

Preparation time: 10 minutes
Cooking time: 15 minutes
Serves: 4

Ingredients To Use:

- 1 pound of red potatoes, wedged
- ½ tap of dried oregano
- 1 pound of green beans
- Salt and black pepper, as desired
- 2 garlic cloves, grated
- 2 Tbsp of olive oil

Step-by-Step Directions to Cook It:

1. Place the cooking pot into the Ninja Foodi Grill, then the crisper basket.

2. Ensure the splatter shield is in position and close the hood.

3. Press the air crisp button. Set the temperature to 380°F and set the time for 15 minutes.

4. Press the start/stop button to preheat the appliance for 3 minutes.

5. Combine the green beans, potatoes, garlic, oil, salt, oregano, and pepper in a bowl.

6. Transfer to the crisper basket and close the hood

Serving suggestions: Serve immediately

Preparation and Cooking Tips: Shake the basket halfway

Nutritional value per serving: Calories: 211kcal, Fat: 6g, Carb: 8g, Proteins: 5g

Air-Crisped Beans and Potatoes

Air-crisped beans and potatoes are delicious and nutritious. It can be served as lunch or dinner.

Preparation time: 10 minutes
Cooking time: 15 minutes
Serves: 5

Ingredients To Use:
- 6 new potatoes, cut into halves
- Salt and black pepper, as desired
- olive oil, a drizzle
- 2 pounds of green beans
- 6 bacon slices, cooked and chopped

Step-by-Step Directions to Cook It:
1. Place the cooking pot into the Ninja Foodi Grill, then the crisper basket.
2. Ensure the splatter shield is in position and close the hood.
3. Press the air crisp button. Set the temperature to 390°F and set the time for 15 minutes.
4. Press the start/stop button to preheat the appliance for 3 minutes.

5. Mix the potatoes, green beans, oil, salt, and pepper in a bowl.

6. Transfer to the crisper basket and close the hood.

Serving suggestions: Serve immediately

Preparation and Cooking Tips: Shake the basket halfway

Nutritional value per serving: Calories: 374kcal, Fat: 15g, Carb: 28g, Proteins: 12g

Stuffed Baby Peppers

Stuffed baby peppers are spicy and delicious. They are healthy and fun to eat.

Preparation time: 10 minutes
Cooking time: 6 minutes
Serves: 4

Ingredients To Use:
- Salt and black pepper, as desired
- 12 baby bell peppers, halved lengthwise
- A handful parsley, chopped
- ¼ tsp red pepper flakes, crumbled
- 1 Tbsp of lemon juice
- 1 pound of shrimp, boiled, deshelled and deveined
- 1 Tbsp of olive oil
- 6 tbsp of jarred basil pesto

Step-by-Step Directions to Cook It:
1. Place the cooking pot into the Ninja Foodi Grill, then the crisper basket.
2. Ensure the splatter shield is in position and close the hood.

3. Press the air crisp button. Set the temperature to 320°F and set the time for 6 minutes.
4. Press the start/stop button to preheat the appliance for 3 minutes.
5. Mix the shrimp, pesto, pepper flakes, parsley, oil, lemon juice, black pepper, and oil in a bowl.
6. Stuff the bell peppers with the mixture
7. Transfer the bell peppers to the crisper basket and close the hood.

Serving suggestions: Serve immediately

Preparation and Cooking Tips: Gently shake the crisper basket

Nutritional value per serving: Calories: 130kcal, Fat: 2g, Carb: 3g, Proteins: 15g

Tomato and Basil Tart

Tomato and basil tart is an exciting meal, it is nutritious and tasty. It can be served as lunch or dinner.
Preparation time: 10 minutes
Cooking time: 14 minutes
Serves: 2

Ingredients To Use:
- 1 bunch basil, sliced
- ¼ cup of grated cheddar cheese
- 4 eggs
- 1 garlic clove, grated
- ½ cup of halved cherry tomatoes
- Salt and black pepper, as desired

Step-by-Step Directions to Cook It:
1. Place the cooking pot into the Ninja Foodi Grill

2. Ensure the splatter shield is in position and close the hood.
3. Press the Bake button. Set the temperature to 320°F and set the time for 14 minutes.
4. Press the start/stop button to preheat the appliance for 3 minutes.
5. Mix the eggs, black pepper, salt, basil, and cheese in a bowl.
6. Transfer the mixture to a baking pan.
7. Top the mixture with tomatoes and transfer the pan to the air fryer.

Serving suggestions: Slice and serve immediately

Preparation and Cooking Tips: Press the Manual button for 2 seconds to view the food's internal temperature.

Nutritional value per serving: Calories: 140kcal, Fat: 1g, Carb: 2g, Proteins: 10g

Chapter 12: Desserts and Snacks

Wrapped Pears

Wrapped pears is a delightful dessert. It excites your taste buds and pleases your senses. It is an amazing treat that makes you crave for more.

Preparation time: 10 minutes
Cooking time: 15 minutes
Serves: 4

Ingredients To Use:
- 14 ounces of vanilla custard
- 4 puff pastry sheets
- 2 pears, halved
- ½ tsp of cinnamon powder
- 1 egg, beaten
- 2 Tbsp of sugar

Step-by-Step Directions to Cook It:
1.   Place the cooking pot into the Ninja Foodi Grill, then the crisper basket.
2.   Ensure the splatter shield is in position and close the hood.
3.   Press the air crisp button. Set the temperature to 320°F and set the time for 15 minutes.
4.   Press the start/stop button to preheat the appliance for 3 minutes.
5.   Place the puff pastries on a flat surface, top with a pear half and a spoon of vanilla custard each.
6.   Wrap the puff pastries.
7.   Brush the pears with the egg, sprinkle with cinnamon and sugar.
8.   Transfer the pastries to the air fryer basket and close the hood.

Serving suggestions: Serve immediately
Preparation and Cooking Tips: Shake the basket periodically
Nutritional value per serving: Calories: 200kcal, Fat: 2g, Carb: 14g, Proteins: 3g

Air-Crisped Banana

Air -crisped are delightful and sumptuous. They' can be enjoyed with other meals.

Preparation time: 10 minutes
Cooking time: 15 minutes
Serves: 4

Ingredients To Use:
- 3 Tbsp of butter, melted
- 1 cup of panko
- 2 eggs
- 8 bananas, unpeeled and cut into halves
- 3 Tbsp of cinnamon sugar
- ½ cup of cornflour

Step-by-Step Directions to Cook It:
1.   Place the cooking pot into the Ninja Foodi Grill, then the crisper basket.
2.   Ensure the splatter shield is in position and close the hood.
3.   Press the air crisp button. Set the temperature to 280°F and set the time for 10 minutes.
4.   Press the start/stop button to preheat the appliance for 3 minutes.

5. Mix the melted butter and panko in a bowl. Mash the bananas and add to the mix

6. Add the flour and eggs to the panko mix and form rolls.

7. Arrange the rolls in the crisper basket and rub them with cinnamon sugar.

8. Close the hood.

Serving suggestions: Serve immediately

Preparation and Cooking Tips: Shake the basket halfway

Nutritional value per serving: Calories: 164kcal, Fat: 1g, Carb: 32g, Proteins: 4g

Lava Cake

Lava cake is an incredible dessert. It is delightful and mouth-watering. It can be enjoyed with ice-cream and drinks.

Preparation time: 10 minutes
Cooking time: 20 minutes
Serves: 3

Ingredients To Use:

- 4 Tbsp of flour
- 1 egg
- 2 Tbsp of olive oil
- ½ Tbsp of orange zest
- 4 Tbsp of milk
- 1 Tbsp of cocoa powder
- 4 Tbsp of sugar
- ½ Tbsp of baking powder

Step-by-Step Directions to Cook It:

1. Place the cooking pot into the Ninja Foodi Grill.

2. Ensure the splatter shield is in position and close the hood.

3. Press the Bake button. Set the temperature to 320°F and set the time for 20 minutes.

4. Press the start/stop button to preheat the appliance for 3 minutes.

5. Mix the eggs and sugar in a bowl.

6. Add milk, flour, cocoa powder, salt, baking powder, and orange zest to the bowl and stir thoroughly.

7. Add the cocoa mix to the ramekins and transfer to the air fryer.

8. Close the hood

Serving suggestions: Serve immediately

Preparation and Cooking Tips: Grease the ramekins before adding the cocoa mix

Nutritional value per serving: Calories: 201kcal, Fat: 7g, Carb: 23g, Proteins: 4g

Air-Crisped Apples

Air-crisped apples are crunchy and delightful. It is easy to prepare and can be enjoyed as lunch.

Preparation time: 10 minutes
Cooking time: 10 minutes
Serves: 4

Ingredients To Use:

- ¾ cup of old-fashioned rolled oats
- 2 tsp of cinnamon powder
- ¼ cup of brown sugar
- 5 apples, pitted and sliced
- ¼ cup of flour
- ½ tsp of nutmeg powder
- 1 Tbsp of maple syrup
- 4 Tbsp of butter

Step-by-Step Directions to Cook It:

1. Place the cooking pot into the Ninja Foodi Grill, then the crisper basket.
2. Ensure the splatter shield is in position and close the hood.
3. Press the air crisp button. Set the temperature to 320°F and set the time for 10 minutes.
4. Press the start/stop button to preheat the appliance for 3 minutes.
5. In a bowl, mix the sugar, oats, salt, flour, butter, cinnamon, nutmeg, and maple syrup.
6. Coat the apple slices with the maple mix and transfer to the crisper basket.
7. Close the hood.

Serving suggestions: Serve immediately

Preparation and Cooking Tips: Shake the basket regularly

Nutritional value per serving: Calories: 200kcal, Fat: 6g, Carb: 29g, Proteins: 12g

Blueberry Scones

Blueberry scone is an elegant and sumptuous dessert. It can be enjoyed with wine or orange juice or any fruit drink of your choice.

Preparation time: 10 minutes
Cooking time: 10 minutes
Serves: 10

Ingredients To Use:
- 1 cup of white flour
- 2 tsp of baking powder
- 1 cup of blueberries
- 2 tsp of vanilla extract
- 2 eggs
- ½ cup of heavy cream
- 5 Tbsp of sugar
- ½ cup of butter

Step-by-Step Directions to Cook It:
1. Place the cooking pot into the Ninja Foodi Grill.
2. Ensure the splatter shield is in position and close the hood.
3. Press the Bake button. Set the temperature to 320°F and set the time for 10 minutes.
4. Press the start/stop button to preheat the appliance for 3 minutes
5. Mix the flour, baking powder, salt, and blueberries in a bowl.
6. In a separate bowl, mix the butter, heavy cream, sugar, vanilla extract, and eggs.
7. Combine the two mixtures and knead until a dough is obtained.
8. Form 10 triangles from the dough and arrange them in the cooking pot.
9. Close the hood

Serving suggestions: Serve the scones cold

Preparation and Cooking Tips: Line the cooking pot with baking sheet before you arrange the dough

Nutritional value per serving: Calories: 130kcal, Fat: 2g, Carb: 4g, Proteins: 3g

Chocolate Cookies

Chocolate cookies have a crunchy and delicious taste. They excite the taste buds and give you a mouth-watering experience.

Preparation time: 10 minutes
Cooking time: 25 minutes
Serves: 12

Ingredients To Use:
- 1 tsp of vanilla extract
- ½ cup of unsweetened chocolate chips
- ½ cup of melted butter
- 2 cups of flour
- 1 egg
- 4 Tbsp of sugar

Step-by-Step Directions to Cook It:
1. Place the cooking pot into the Ninja Foodi Grill.
2. Ensure the splatter shield is in position and close the hood.
3. Press the Bake button. Set the temperature to 330°F and set the time for 25 minutes.
4. Press the start/stop button to preheat the appliance for 3 minutes.
5. Mix the egg, sugar, vanilla extract in a bowl.
6. Add the flour, melted butter, and ½ chocolate chips
7. Whisk thoroughly and pour into a baking pan.
8. Top with the rest of the chocolate chips
9. Close the hood

Serving suggestions: Serve cold
Preparation and Cooking Tips: grease the baking pan with cooking spray before adding the flour mix.
Nutritional value per serving: Calories: 230kcal, Fat: 12g, Carb: 4g, Proteins: 5g

Macaroons

Macaroons are sweet and have a unique taste. They are easy to make and can be enjoyed at any time of the day.

Preparation time: 10 minutes
Cooking time: 8 minutes
Serves: 20
Ingredients To Use:
- 2 Tbsp of sugar
- 1 tsp of vanilla extract
- 4 egg whites
- 2 cup of shredded coconut

Step-by-Step Directions to Cook It:
1. Place the cooking pot into the Ninja Foodi Grill, then the crisper basket.
2. Ensure the splatter shield is in position and close the hood.
3. Press the air crisper button. Set the temperature to 340°F and set the time for 8 minutes.
4. Press the start/stop button to preheat the appliance for 3 minutes.
5. Mix the egg whites and stevia in a bowl.
6. Add the vanilla extract and shredded coconut to the bowl.
7. Form balls with the mix and transfer them to the crisper basket.
8. Close the hood

Serving suggestions: Serve cold
Preparation and Cooking Tips: Shake the basket halfway
Nutritional value per serving: Calories: 55kcal, Fat: 6g, Carb: 2g, Proteins: 1g

Date Brownies and Lentils

This recipe results in a special kind of cake with an awesome taste. The cake tastes delightful and can be enjoyed with any fruit drink.
Preparation time: 10 minutes
Cooking time: 15 minutes

Serves: 8

Ingredients To Use:
- 28 ounces of canned lentils, drained
- 2 Tbsp of cocoa powder
- 12 dates
- 4 Tbsp of almond butter
- 1 Tbsp of honey
- ½ tsp baking soda
- 1 banana, unpeeled and sliced

Step-by-Step Directions to Cook It:
1. Place the cooking pot into the Ninja Foodi Grill.
2. Ensure the splatter shield is in position and close the hood.
3. Press the Bake button. Set the temperature to 360°F and set the time for 15 minutes.
4. Press the start/stop button to preheat the appliance for 3 minutes.
5. Add the lentils, butter, honey, baking soda to the food processor and blend until smooth.
6. Add the dates and pulse well.
7. Transfer the blended mix to the baking pan. Spread evenly.
8. Transfer the baking pan to the air fryer and close the hood.

Serving suggestions: Cut up the brownies and serve

Preparation and Cooking Tips: Follow the cooking directions fastidiously

Nutritional value per serving: Calories: 162kcal, Fat: 4g, Carb: 3g, Proteins: 4g

Maple Cupcakes

Maple cupcakes are delicious. You can enjoy it with a cup of tea.
Preparation time: 10 minutes

Cooking time: 20 minutes
Serves: 4

Ingredients To Use:
- 1 tsp of vanilla extract
- 4 Tbsp of melted butter
- ½ tsp of baking powder
- 4 eggs
- ¾ cup of white flour
- 4 tsp of maple syrup
- ½ cup of pure applesauce
- ½ apple, cored and chopped
- 2 tsp of cinnamon powder

Step-by-Step Directions to Cook It:
1. Place the cooking pot into the Ninja Foodi Grill.
2. Ensure the splatter shield is in position and close the hood.
3. Press the Bake button. Set the temperature to 350°F and set the time for 20 minutes.
4. Press the start/stop button to preheat the appliance for 3 minutes.
5. Mix the melted butter, applesauce, eggs, maple syrup, and vanilla in a bowl
6. Add the flour, cinnamon, apples, and baking powder. Whisk.
7. Transfer the batter to the cupcake pan and place it in the air fryer.
8. Close the hood.

Serving suggestions: Serve cold

Preparation and Cooking Tips: grease the pan before adding to the cupcake pan

Nutritional value per serving: Calories: 150kcal, Fat: 3g, Carb: 5g, Proteins: 4g

Mandarin Pudding

Mandarin pudding is delicious and nutritious. It is made of mandarin fruit, which is also responsible for providing vitamins to the body.

Preparation time: 20 minutes
Cooking time: 20 minutes
Serves: 8

Ingredients To Use:

- 1 mandarin, peeled and sliced
- A drizzle of honey
- 2 mandarins, juiced
- ¾ cup of ground almonds
- ¾ cup of white flour
- 2 Tbsp of brown sugar
- ¾ cup of sugar
- 4 ounces of soft butter
- 2 eggs, beaten

Step-by-Step Directions to Cook It:

1. Place the cooking pot into the Ninja Foodi Grill.
2. Ensure the splatter shield is in position and close the hood.
3. Press the Bake button. Set the temperature to 360°F and set the time for 40 minutes.
4. Press the start/stop button to preheat the appliance for 3 minutes.
5. Grease the baking pan with butter. Sprinkle with sugar.
6. Arrange the mandarin slices in the baking pan.
7. Mix the butter, sugar, almonds, eggs, mandarin juice, and flour in a bowl.
8. Spoon the egg mix over the mandarin slices and transfer the pan to the air fryer.
9. Close the hood

Serving suggestions: Transfer to a plate and top with honey

Preparation and Cooking Tips: Grease the loaf pan at the start.
Nutritional value per serving: Calories: 162kcal, Fat: 3g, Carb: 3g, Proteins:6 g

Sponge Cake

Sponge cake is a delightful dessert. It is mouth-watering and excites the taste bud. It can be enjoyed at any time of the day.

Preparation time: 10 minutes
Cooking time: 20 minutes
Serves: 12

Ingredients To Use:

- 2 tsp of vanilla extract
- 3 tsp of baking powder
- 3 cups of flour
- ½ cup of cornstarch
- 1 cup of olive oil
- 1 tsp of baking soda
- 1½ cup of milk
- 2 cups of water
- 12/3 cup sugar
- ¼ cup of lemon juice

Step-by-Step Directions to Cook It:

1. Place the cooking pot into the Ninja Foodi Grill and ensure the splatter shield is in position. Close the hood.
2. Press the Bake button. Use the default temperature of 350°F and set the time for 20 minutes.
3. Press the start/stop button to preheat the appliance for 3 minutes.
4. Mix the flour, cornstarch, baking soda, baking powder, and sugar in a bowl.

5. In a separate bowl, mix the milk, oil, water, lemon juice, and vanilla in a bowl.
6. Combine both mixtures and transfer to a baking pan.
7. Close the hood.

Serving suggestions: Serve Cold
Preparation and Cooking Tips: Grease the baking pan before adding the mixtures
Nutritional value per serving: Calories: 246kcal, Fat: 3g, Carb: 6g, Proteins: 2g

Ricotta and Lemon cake

Ricotta and lemon cake can be enjoyed at any time of the day. It is delicious and filling.
Preparation time: 10 minutes
Cooking time: 70 minutes
Serves: 4
Ingredients To Use:
- ½ pound of sugar
- 1 orange, zested and grated
- 8 eggs, beaten
- Butter
- 3 pounds of ricotta cheese
- 1 lemon, zested and grated

Step-by-Step Directions to Cook It:
1. Place the cooking pot into the Ninja Foodi Grill and ensure the splatter shield is in position. Close the hood.
2. Press the Bake button. Use the default temperature of 380°F and set the time for 40 minutes.
3. Press the start/stop button to preheat the appliance for 3 minutes.

4. Mix the eggs, cheese, sugar, orange, and lemon zest in a bowl.
5. Spread the egg mix in a baking pan and transfer to the air fryer.
6. Close the hood.
Serving suggestions: Allow to cool before serving
Preparation and Cooking Tips: Grease the baking pan with butter before adding the egg mix
Nutritional value per serving: Calories: 110kcal, Fat: 3g, Carb: 3g, Proteins: 4g

Tangerine Cake

Tangerine cake is a healthy dessert that provides the body with vitamins. It is delicious and can be enjoyed as dessert at any time of the day.
Preparation time: 10 minutes
Cooking time: 20 minutes
Serves: 8
Ingredients To Use:
- ¾ cup of sugar
- 2 cups of flour
- ¼ cup of olive oil
- ½ cup of milk
- 1 tsp of cider vinegar
- ½ tsp of vanilla extract
- 2 lemons, juiced and zested
- 1 tangerine, juiced and zested
- Tangerine segments

Step-by-Step Directions to Cook It:
1. Place the cooking pot into the Ninja Foodi Grill and ensure the splatter shield is in position. Close the hood.
2. Press the Bake button. Use the default temperature of 360°F and set the time for 20 minutes.

3. Press the start/stop button to preheat the appliance for 3 minutes.
4. Mix the milk, oil, vinegar, lemon juice, vanilla extract, lemon, and tangerine zest.
5. Add the flour, whisk thoroughly and transfer this to a baking pan.
6. Add the baking pan to the preheated air fryer and close the hood

Serving suggestions: Top with tangerine segments

Preparation and Cooking Tips: Grease the baking pan before adding the mix

Nutritional value per serving: Calories: 190kcal, Fat: 1g, Carb: 4g, Proteins: 4g

Blueberry Pudding

Blueberry pudding is an elegant dessert. It is beautiful and have got a delightful and fruity taste.
Preparation time: 10 minutes
Cooking time: 25 minutes
Serves: 6

Ingredients To Use:
- 1 cup of chopped walnuts
- 2 cups of flour
- 3 Tbsp of maple syrup
- 2 cups of rolled oats
- 8 cups of blueberries
- 2 Tbsp of chopped rosemary
- 1 stick of melted butter

Step-by-Step Directions to Cook It:
1. Place the cooking pot into the Ninja Foodi Grill and ensure the splatter shield is in position. Close the hood.

2. Press the Bake button. Use the default temperature of 350°F and set the time for 25 minutes.
3. Press the start/stop button to preheat the appliance for 3 minutes.
4. Spread the blueberries in a baking pan. Set aside
5. Blend the flour, oats, butter, walnuts, maple syrup, and rosemary with a food processor.
6. Transfer the mixture to the baking pan, the air fryer.
7. Close the hood.

Serving suggestions: Allow to cool before cutting and serving

Preparation and Cooking Tips: Grease the baking pan before adding the blueberries

Nutritional value per serving: Calories: 150kcal, Fat: 3g, Carb: 7g, Proteins: 4g

Cocoa and Almond Bars

Cocoa and almond bar is a perfect dessert for vegans. It is delicious, fun to eat, and can be enjoyed with any fruit drink.
Preparation time: 30 minutes
Cooking time: 40 minutes
Serves: 6

Ingredients To Use:
- ¼ cup of shredded coconut
- ¼ cup of cocoa nibs
- 8 dates, pitted and soaked
- 1 cup of soaked almonds, drained
- 2 Tbsp of cocoa powder
- ¼ cup of goji berries
- ¼ cup of hemp seeds

Step-by-Step Directions to Cook It:

1.   Place the cooking pot into the Ninja Foodi Grill and ensure the splatter shield is in position. Close the hood.

2.   Press the Bake button. Use the default temperature of 320°F and set the time for 4 minutes.

3.   Press the start/stop button to preheat the appliance for 3 minutes.

4.   Blend the almonds, cocoa nibs, goji berries, coconut, cocoa powder, coconut, and hemp seeds with your food processor.

5.   Add the dates and pulse until smooth.

6.   Spread the blended mixture on the cooking pot and close the hood.

Serving suggestions: Cut into 6 parts and cool in the fridge for 30 minutes before serving

Preparation and Cooking Tips: Line the cooking pot with a baking sheet for best baking

Nutritional value per serving: Calories: 140kcal, Fat: 6g, Carb: 7g, Proteins: 19g

Chapter 13: Game Recipes

Foodi Pheasant Legs

Pheasant legs are delicious and fun to eat. The meal provides the body with necessary nutrients and can be enjoyed as lunch or dinner.

Preparation time: 10 minutes
Cooking time: 36 minutes
Serves: 2

Ingredients To Use:
- 2 pheasant legs
- 2 dried chilies, chopped
- 2 star anises
- 1 Tbsp of olive oil
- 1 bunch spring onions, chopped
- 4 ginger slices
- 1 Tbsp of soy sauce
- 1 Tbsp of oyster sauce
- 1 tsp of sesame oil
- 14 ounces of water
- 1 Tbsp of rice wine

Step-by-Step Directions to Cook It:
1. Place the cooking pot into the Ninja Foodi Grill and ensure the splatter shield is in position. Close the hood.
2. Press the Bake button. Set the temperature to 370°F and adjust the time to 30 minutes.
3. Press the start/stop button to preheat the appliance for 3 minutes.
4. Combine the chili, star anise, rice wine, sesame oil, oyster sauce, ginger, and water in a bowl.
5. Add the pheasant legs and spring onions. Toss until well coated.

6. Transfer the contents of the bowl to the cooking pot and close the hood.

Serving suggestions: Serve immediately

Preparation and Cooking Tips: Stir the food halfway

Nutritional value per serving: Calories: 300kcal, Fat: 12g, Carb: 26g, Proteins: 18g

Air-Crisped Venison Steaks and Apple Sauce

Air-crisped venison steaks and apple sauce is an exciting meal; it excites the taste buds and provides the body with vital nutrients.

Preparation time: 10 minutes
Cooking time: 40 minutes
Serves: 6

Ingredients To Use:
- 2 Tbsp of sugar
- A drizzle of olive oil
- 1 Tbsp of lemon juice
- 17 ounces apples, seeded and quartered
- 1 quart of water
- 3 venison steaks, chopped into medium pieces
- Salt and black pepper, as desired

Step-by-Step Directions to Cook It:
1. Place the cooking pot into the Ninja Foodi Grill, then the crisper basket.
2. Ensure the splatter shield is in position and close the hood.

3. Press the air crisp button. Set the temperature to 400°F and set the time for 40 minutes.
4. Press the start/stop button to preheat the appliance for 3 minutes.
5. Blend the apples, sugar, and lemon juice with a food processor.
6. Mix the meat with the blended mixture in a bowl.
7. Transfer the coated meat to the cooking pot and close the hood.
8. After 25 minutes, add the sauce to the cooking pot and close the hood.

Serving suggestions: Serve the venison with the sauce

Preparation and Cooking Tips: Stir the food halfway

Nutritional value per serving: Calories: 456kcal, Fat: 34g, Carb: 10g, Proteins: 25g

Easy Pheasant Breasts

Pheasant breast is a savory meal. It can be served as dinner or lunch. It is nutritious.
Preparation time: 10 minutes
Cooking time: 40 minutes
Serves: 6

Ingredients To Use:
- 3 Tbsp of flour
- 2 cups of chicken stock
- ½ cup of white wine
- Salt and black pepper, as desired
- ¼ cup of chopped parsley
- 6 pheasant breasts, halved
- 6 Tbsp of melted butter
- 2 cups of chopped mushrooms

Step-by-Step Directions to Cook It:

1. Place the cooking pot into the Ninja Foodi Grill and ensure the splatter shield is in position. Close the hood.
2. Press the Bake button. Set the temperature to 350°F and adjust the time to 40 minutes.
3. Press the start/stop button to preheat the appliance for 3 minutes.
4. Season the pheasant breast with pepper and salt.
5. Combine the melted butter, wine, flour, pepper, salt in another bowl and add the pheasant.
6. Transfer all the contents of the bowl to the cooking pot and close the hood.

Serving suggestions: Serve immediately

Preparation and Cooking Tips: Stir the food halfway

Nutritional value per serving: Calories: 320kcal, Fat: 28g, Carb: 12g, Proteins: 42g

Venison and Cherries

Venison and cherries taste great. It can be served as lunch or dinner.
Preparation time: minutes
Cooking time: minutes
Serves:

Ingredients To Use:
- 4 venison steaks
- ½ cup of sugar
- 1/3 cup of balsamic vinegar
- ¼ cup of honey
- 1 tsp of garlic, grated
- 1 tsp of ground cumin
- 1 Tbsp of ginger, minced
- ½ tsp of ground clove

- 4 sage leaves, chopped
- ½ tsp of cinnamon powder
- 1 jalapeno, chopped
- ½ cup of chopped yellow onion
- 2 cups of sliced rhubarb
- 2 cups of pitted cherries

Step-by-Step Directions to Cook It:

1. Place the cooking pot and grill plate into the Ninja Foodi Grill and ensure the splatter shield is positioned. Close the hood.
2. Press the grill button. Set the temperature to 350°F and adjust the time to 10 minutes.
3. Press the start/stop button to preheat the appliance for 3 minutes.
4. Season the venison with pepper and salt.
5. Transfer to the grill plate and close the hood.
6. Meanwhile, combine the sugar, honey, ginger, vinegar, cumin, sage, clove, rhubarb, jalapeno, vinegar, cinnamon, garlic, sage onions, and cherries in a bowl.
7. When the venison is done grilling, remove the grill plate, then add the cherry mix to the cooking pot. Include the venison.
8. Press the bake button and set the time to 10 minutes at the same temperature

Serving suggestions: Serve the steaks and drizzle with the sauce

Preparation and Cooking Tips: Flip the venison halfway during the grilling

Nutritional value per serving: Calories: 456kcal, Fat: 13g, Carb: 64g, Proteins: 31g

Venison and Tea Sauce

Venison and tea sauce is an awesome meal. It provides the body with vital nutrients and can be enjoyed as dinner or lunch.

Preparation time: 10 minutes
Cooking time: 20 minutes
Serves: 4

Ingredients To Use:

- 1½ cup of orange juice
- 1 Tbsp of honey
- 2 venison steaks
- 3 tsp of earl gray tea leaves
- 2¼ cup chicken stock
- Salt and black pepper, as desired
- ¾ cup of chopped shallot
- 3 Tbsp of melted butter

Step-by-Step Directions to Cook It:

1. Place the cooking pot into the Ninja Foodi Grill and ensure the splatter shield is in position. Close the hood.
2. Press the Bake button. Set the temperature to 360°F and adjust the time to 20 minutes.
3. Press the start/stop button to preheat the appliance for 3 minutes.
4. Season the venison steaks with salt and pepper, then transfer to the preheated air fryer.
5. After 10 minutes, add the stock.
6. After 2 minutes, add the orange juice and stir.
7. After 3 minutes, add the shallots, butter, tea leaves, and honey.
8. Leave to cook for the rest of the 3 minutes

Serving suggestions: Serve the venison drizzled with the tea sauce
Preparation and Cooking Tips: Stir the food regularly.
Nutritional value per serving: Calories: 228kcal, Fat: 11g, Carb: 20g, Proteins: 12g

Pheasant and Beer Sauce

Pheasant and beer sauce is a tasty meal with a unique taste. It is nutritious.
Preparation time: 15 minutes
Cooking time: 45 minutes
Serves: 6
Ingredients To Use:
- 1 cup of dark beer
- 1 whole pheasant, cut into small pieces
- 1 dried Portobello mushroom
- 1 yellow onion, chopped
- 6 thyme springs, chopped
- 1 bay leaf
- Salt and black pepper, as desired
- 1 cup of chicken stock
- ¼ cup of tomato paste

Step-by-Step Directions to Cook It:
1. Place the cooking pot into the Ninja Foodi Grill and ensure the splatter shield is in position. Close the hood.
2. Press the Bake button. Set the temperature to 350°F and adjust the time to 40 minutes.
3. Press the start/stop button to preheat the appliance for 3 minutes.
4. Combine the tomato paste, beer, mushroom, onion, thyme and bay leaves in a bowl.

5. Add the pheasant and stir.
6. Transfer to the cooking pot and close the hood
Serving suggestions: Serve hot
Preparation and Cooking Tips: Stir the food halfway
Nutritional value per serving: Calories: 300kcal, Fat: 7g, Carb: 18g, Proteins: 23g

Creamy Venison

Creamy venison is a tasty meal; it provides the body with necessary nutrients. It can be served as dinner or lunch.
Preparation time: 10 minutes
Cooking time: 22 minutes
Serves: 6
Ingredients To Use:
- 2 Tbsp of chopped dill
- 4 venison steaks, boneless and cubed
- 1 Tbsp of olive oil
- 2 yellow onions, chopped
- 3 cups of chicken stock
- 1 garlic clove, minced
- 2 Tbsp of sweet paprika
- 2 Tbsp of white flour
- Salt and black pepper, as desired
- 1½ cups of sour cream

Step-by-Step Directions to Cook It:
1. Place the cooking pot into the Ninja Foodi Grill and ensure the splatter shield is in position. Close the hood.
2. Press the Bake button. Set the temperature to 370°F and adjust the time to 15 minutes.

3. Press the start/stop button to preheat the appliance for 3 minutes.
4. Season the venison with salt, pepper, and oil.
5. Transfer to the cooking pot
6. Add the stock, paprika, sour cream, flour, dill, garlic, and onion.
7. Close the hood.
Serving suggestions: Serve immediately
Preparation and Cooking Tips: Stir the food halfway
Nutritional value per serving: Calories: 450kcal, Fat: 10g, Carb: 31g, Proteins: 39g

Pheasant Roast and Wine Sauce

Pheasant roast and wine sauce taste great. It is an elegant meal that can be served as dinner or lunch.
Preparation time: 10 minutes
Cooking time: 45 minutes
Serves: 6
Ingredients To Use:
- 5 potatoes, chopped
- 1 whole pheasant, chopped into medium pieces
- 4 garlic cloves, minced
- Salt and black pepper, as desired
- 1 yellow onion, chopped
- 17 ounces of beef stock
- ½ tsp of smoked paprika
- ½ tsp of chicken salt
- 3 ounces of red wine
- 3 carrots, chopped
Step-by-Step Directions to Cook It:
1. Place the cooking pot into the Ninja Foodi Grill and ensure the

splatter shield is in position. Close the hood.
2. Press the Bake button. Set the temperature to 360°F and adjust the time to 45 minutes.
3. Press the start/stop button to preheat the appliance for 3 minutes.
4. Mix the pepper, pheasant, salt, chicken salt, and paprika in a bowl.
5. Add the onion, stock, wine, garlic, carrots, and potatoes to the bowl.
6. Pour the contents of the bowl into the cooking pot and close the hood.
Serving suggestions: Serve hot
Preparation and Cooking Tips: Stir the food halfway
Nutritional value per serving: Calories: 304kcal, Fat: 20g, Carb: 20g, Proteins: 32g

Venison Curry

Venison curry is a delicious and healthy meal. It can be enjoyed as lunch or dinner.
Preparation time: 10 minutes
Cooking time: 45 minutes
Serves: 4
Ingredients To Use:
- 2 pounds of venison steak, cubed
- 3 potatoes, cubed
- 2 Tbsp of olive oil
- 1 Tbsp of wine mustard
- 2 yellow onions, chopped
- 2 garlic cloves, minced
- 2½ Tbsp of curry powder
- 2 Tbsp of tomato sauce

- 10 ounces of canned coconut milk
- Salt and black pepper, as desired

Step-by-Step Directions to Cook It:

1. Place the cooking pot into the Ninja Foodi Grill and ensure the splatter shield is in position. Close the hood.
2. Press the Bake button. Set the temperature to 360°F and adjust the time to 40 minutes.
3. Press the start/stop button to preheat the appliance for 3 minutes.
4. Mix the onions and garlic in a bowl.
5. Add the potatoes and mustard.
6. Add the venison, coconut milk, salt, pepper, curry powder, and tomato sauce to the bowl.
7. Transfer the contents of the bowl to the cooking pot and close the hood.

Serving suggestions: Serve immediately

Preparation and Cooking Tips: Stir the food halfway

Nutritional value per serving: Calories: 432kcal, Fat: 16g, Carb: 20g, Proteins: 27g

Pheasant and Raspberry Sauce

Pheasant and raspberry sauce is an elegant meal; it is nutritious and is best enjoyed as dinner.

Preparation time: 10 minutes
Cooking time: 15 minutes
Serves: 4

Ingredients To Use:

- ½ cup of water
- Salt and black pepper, as desired
- Cooking spray
- 2 pheasant breasts, skin on and scored
- ½ tsp of cinnamon powder
- ½ cup of raspberries
- 1 tsp of red wine vinegar
- 1 Tbsp of sugar

Step-by-Step Directions to Cook It:

1. Place the cooking pot into the Ninja Foodi AG301, and position the grill plate with the handles facing up.
2. Ensure the splatter shield is in position. Close the hood.
3. Press the Grill button. Set the temperature to 350°F and adjust the time to 10 minutes.
4. Season the pheasant breasts with pepper and salt.
5. Transfer the pheasant to the grill plate and close the hood.
6. When the time is up, remove the grill plate and return the pheasant to the cooking pot.
7. Add the wine, water, raspberries, sugar, and cinnamon to the cooking pot and close the hood. Increase the timer by 4 minutes.
8. Separate the sauce from the pheasants and blend the sauce with a food processor
9. Divide the pheasants into four portions and top with the blended raspberry puree.

Serving suggestions: Serve immediately

Preparation and Cooking Tips: Stir the food halfway

Chapter 14: Grilling Recipes

Coconut Tilapia

Tasty pollock is delicious and nutritious. It can be best served as dinner.
Preparation time: 10 minutes
Cooking time: 15 minutes
Serves: 6

Ingredients To Use:
- 4 boneless Pollock fillets
- ½ cup of sour cream
- ¼ cup of grated parmesan
- Salt and black pepper, as desired
- 2 Tbsp of melted butter
- Cooking spray

Step-by-Step Directions to Cook It:
1. Place the cooking pot into the Ninja Foodi AG301, and position the grill plate with the handles facing up.
2. Ensure the splatter shield is in position. Close the hood.
3. Press the Grill button. Set the temperature to 320°F and adjust the time to 15 minutes. Press the start/stop button to preheat the appliance for 8 minutes.
4. Mix the butter, sour cream, salt, parmesan, and pepper in a bowl.
5. Spray the fish with the cooking spray and rub with salt and pepper.
6. Coat both sides of the fish with the sour cream mix and arrange on the grill plate.
7. Close the hood
 Serving suggestions: Serve immediately with salad

Preparation and Cooking Tips: Flip the items on the grill plate halfway
Nutritional value per serving: Calories: 300kcal, Fat: 13g, Carb: 14g, Proteins: 44g

Coconut Tilapia

Coconut tilapia has got a unique and delicious taste. It provides vital nutrients to the body and can be enjoyed as lunch.
Preparation time: 10 minutes
Cooking time: 10 minutes
Serves: 4

Ingredients To Use:
- Cooking spray
- Salt and black pepper, as desired
- 1 tsp of grated ginger
- ½ cup of coconut milk
- ½ cup of chopped cilantro
- ½ tsp of garam masala
- 2 garlic cloves, minced
- 4 medium tilapia fillets
- ½ jalapeno, chopped

Step-by-Step Directions to Cook It:
1. Place the cooking pot into the Ninja Foodi AG301, and position the grill plate with the handles facing up.
2. Ensure the splatter shield is in position. Close the hood.
3. Press the Grill button. Set the temperature to 400°F and adjust the time to 10 minutes. Press the start/stop

button to preheat the appliance for 8 minutes.

4.   Blend the coconut milk, cilantro, salt, pepper, garlic, jalapeno, garam masala, and ginger with a food processor.

5.   Spray the fish with the cooking spray and coat with the coconut mix.

6.   Transfer to the grill plate and close the hood.

Serving suggestions: Serve immediately

Preparation and Cooking Tips: Flip the items on the grill plate halfway

Nutritional value per serving: Calories: 200kcal, Fat: 5g, Carb: 25g, Proteins: 26g

Oriental Red Snapper

Oriental red snapper is an exciting dish. It is nutritious and delicious.
Preparation time: 10 minutes
Cooking time: 12 minutes
Serves:

Ingredients To Use:
- 1 Tbsp of lemon juice
- 2 pounds of boneless red snapper fillets
- 3 garlic cloves, grated
- 1 Tbsp of tamarind paste
- 1 yellow onion, chopped
- 1 Tbsp of oriental sesame oil
- 2 Tbsp of water
- 1 Tbsp of grated ginger
- ½ tsp of ground cumin
- Salt and black pepper, as desired
- 3 Tbsp of chopped mint

Step-by-Step Directions to Cook It:

1.   Place the cooking pot into the Ninja Foodi AG301, and position the grill plate with the handles facing up.

2.   Ensure the splatter shield is in position. Close the hood.

3.   Press the Grill button. Set the temperature to 320°F and adjust the time to 12 minutes. Press the start/stop button to preheat the appliance for 8 minutes.

4.   Blend the ginger, cumin, sesame oil, tamarind paste, pepper, salt, and onion with a food processor.

5.   Coat the fish with the blended mixture and transfer to the grill plate.

6.   Close the hood.

7.   Serve immediately

Serving suggestions: Drizzle fish with lemon and top with mint.

Preparation and Cooking Tips: Flip the items on the grill plate halfway

Nutritional value per serving: Calories: 241kcal, Fat: 8g, Carb: 17g, Proteins: 12g

Snapper Fillets and Veggies

Snapper fillets and veggies is a healthy meal that provides the body with healthy benefits.
Preparation time: 10 minutes
Cooking time: 14 minutes
Serves: 2

Ingredients To Use:
- 2 red boneless snapper fillets
- ½ cup of chopped green bell pepper
- 1 Tbsp of olive oil
- ½ cup of chopped red bell pepper
- ½ cup of chopped leeks

- Salt and black pepper, as desired
- 1 tsp of dried tarragon,
- A splash of white wine

Step-by-Step Directions to Cook It:

1. Place the cooking pot into the Ninja Foodi AG301, and position the grill plate with the handles facing up.
2. Ensure the splatter shield is in position. Close the hood.
3. Press the Grill button. Set the temperature to 350°F and adjust the time to 14 minutes. Press the start/stop button to preheat the appliance for 8 minutes.
4. Season the fish with pepper, oil, salt, tarragon, leeks, red bell pepper, green bell pepper, leeks, wine, and tarragon.
5. Transfer to the grill plate and close the hood.
6. Divide the fish and veggies into plates

  Serving suggestions: Serve immediately

Preparation and Cooking Tips: Flip the items on the grill plate halfway

Nutritional value per serving: Calories: 300kcal, Fat: 12g, Carb: 29g, Proteins: 12g

Marinated Salmon

Marinated salmon is delicious and healthy. Best served as dinner.
Preparation time: 60 minutes
Cooking time: 20 minutes
Serves: 6

Ingredients To Use:

- 1 Tbsp of chopped dill
- 1 whole salmon

- 1 lemon, sliced
- 1 Tbsp of grated garlic
- 1 Tbsp of chopped tarragon
- 2 lemons, juiced
- salt and black pepper, as desired

Step-by-Step Directions to Cook It:

1. Place the cooking pot into the Ninja Foodi AG301, and position the grill plate with the handles facing up.
2. Ensure the splatter shield is in position. Close the hood.
3. Press the Grill button. Set the temperature to 320°F and adjust the time to 25 minutes. Press the start/stop button to preheat the appliance for 8 minutes.
4. Season the fish with salt, lemon juice, and pepper.
5. Marinate fish in the fridge for 1 hour.
6. Stuff the fish with lemon slices and garlic.
7. Transfer to the grill plate and close the hood.

  Serving suggestions: Serve immediately with coleslaw

Preparation and Cooking Tips: Flip the items on the grill plate halfway

Nutritional value per serving: Calories: 300kcal, Fat: 8g, Carb: 19g, Proteins: 27g

Foodi Grilled Cod

Grilled cod is an amazing dish. Tasty and nutritious.
Preparation time: minutes
Cooking time: minutes
Serves:

Ingredients To Use:

- 2 medium, boneless cod fillets
- ½ tsp of grated ginger
- 1 tsp of crushed peanuts
- 1 Tbsp of light soy sauce
- 2 tsp of garlic powder

Step-by-Step Directions to Cook It:

1. Place the cooking pot into the Ninja Foodi AG301, and position the grill plate with the handles facing up.
2. Ensure the splatter shield is in position. Close the hood.
3. Press the Grill button. Set the temperature to 350°F and adjust the time to 10 minutes. Press the start/stop button to preheat the appliance for 8 minutes.
4. Season the fish with garlic, say sauce, and ginger.
5. Transfer to the grill plate and close the hood.

Serving suggestions: Top with peanuts and serve immediately

Preparation and Cooking Tips: Flip the items on the grill plate halfway

Nutritional value per serving: Calories: 254kcal, Fat: 10g, Carb: 14g, Proteins: 23g

Pork Chops and Sage Sauce

Pork chops and sage sauce is an enjoyable meal. It is nutritious and best served as dinner

Preparation time: 10 minutes
Cooking time: 15 minutes
Serves: 2

Ingredients To Use:

- 1 shallot, sliced
- 1 Tbsp of olive oil
- 2 Tbsp of melted butter
- 1 tsp of lemon juice

- 2 pork chops
- Salt and pepper, as desired
- 1 handful sage, chopped

Step-by-Step Directions to Cook It:

1. Place the cooking pot into the Ninja Foodi AG301, and position the grill plate with the handles facing up.
2. Ensure the splatter shield is in position. Close the hood.
3. Press the Grill button. Set the temperature to 370°F and adjust the time to 10 minutes. Press the start/stop button to preheat the appliance for 8 minutes.
4. Season the pork with salt, pepper, and oil.
5. Transfer the pork to the grill plate and close the hood.
6. In a separate bowl, combine the butter, shallot, sage juice, and lemon juice.
7. Remove the grill plate and chicken, then add the sage mix to the cooking pot
8. Close the hood, press the bake button, set the timer for 5 minutes at the same temperature, and press the start button.
9. Drizzle pork with sage sauce.

Serving suggestions: Serve immediately

Preparation and Cooking Tips: Flip the items on the grill plate halfway

Nutritional value per serving: Calories: 265kcal, Fat: 6g, Carb: 19g, Proteins: 12g

Grilled Chicken and Chili Sauce

Grilled chicken and chili sauce is tasty and fun to eat. It is nutritious.

Preparation time: 10 minutes
Cooking time: 20 minutes
Serves: 6

Ingredients To Use:
- 2 cups of ketchup
- 2 cups of chili sauce
- 1 cup of pear jelly
- ½ tsp of liquid smoke
- ¼ cup of honey
- 1 tsp of chili powder
- 1 tsp of mustard powder
- 1 tsp of sweet paprika
- 1 tsp of garlic powder
- Salt and black pepper, as desired
- 6 chicken breasts, skinless and boneless

Step-by-Step Directions to Cook It:
1. Place the cooking pot into the Ninja Foodi AG301, and position the grill plate with the handles facing up.
2. Ensure the splatter shield is in position. Close the hood.
3. Press the Grill button. Set the temperature to 350°F and adjust the time to 10 minutes. Press the start/stop button to preheat the appliance for 8 minutes.
4. Season the chicken with salt and pepper.
5. Arrange the seasoned chicken on the grill plate and close the hood.
6. In a separate bowl, combine the chili sauce, ketchup, honey, liquid smoke, mustard, pear jelly, mustard powder, salt, pepper, paprika, and garlic powder.
7. Remove the chicken and the grill plate from the appliance and add the sauce to the cooking pot.

8. Close the hood, press the bake button, set the time for 10 minutes at the same temperature, and press the start button.
9. Serve the roasted chicken with the sauce

Serving suggestions: Serve immediately
Preparation and Cooking Tips: Flip the items on the grill plate halfway
Nutritional value per serving: Calories: 373kcal, Fat: 13g, Carb: 39g, Proteins: 33g

Foodi Special Pork Chops

Special pork chops are chewy and tasty. The meal can be best served as dinner.

Preparation time: 10 minutes
Cooking time: 15 minutes
Serves: 4

Ingredients To Use:
- 3 garlic cloves, grated
- 4 pork chops
- 1 Tbsp of chopped sage
- 2 Tbsp of olive oil
- Salt and black pepper, as desired
- 2 Tbsp of chopped parsley
- 16 ounces of green beans

Step-by-Step Directions to Cook It:
1. Place the cooking pot into the Ninja Foodi AG301, and position the grill plate with the handles facing up.
2. Ensure the splatter shield is in position. Close the hood.
3. Press the Grill button. Set the temperature to 3600°F and adjust the time to 15 minutes. Press the start/stop

button to preheat the appliance for 8 minutes.

4.   Mix the pork chops with sage, oil, salt, parsley, garlic, and pepper.

5.   Transfer the contents of the bowl to the grill plate and close the hood

Serving suggestions: Serve immediately

Preparation and Cooking Tips: Flip the items on the grill plate halfway

Nutritional value per serving: Calories: 261kcal, Fat: 7g, Carb: 14g, Proteins: 20g

Foodi Grilled Potatoes

Grilled potatoes are perfect as snacks on cold days. Warm yourself with Ninja Foodi Grilled potatoes
Preparation time: 10 minutes
Cooking time: 15 minutes
Serves: 4

Ingredients To Use:
- red pepper flakes, a pinch
- 3 sweet potatoes, quartered
- 2 green onions, sliced
- 4 Tbsp of olive oil
- 2 Tbsp of balsamic vinegar
- 4 garlic cloves, grated
- ½ pound of chopped bacon
- Salt and black pepper, as desired

- 1 lime, juiced
- A handful of chopped dill
- cinnamon powder, a pinch

Step-by-Step Directions to Cook It:

1.   Place the cooking pot into the Ninja Foodi AG301, and position the grill plate with the handles facing up.

2.   Ensure the splatter shield is in position. Close the hood.

3.   Press the Grill button. Set the temperature to 350°F and adjust the time to 15 minutes. Press the start/stop button to preheat the appliance for 8 minutes.

4.   Season the bacon and sweet potatoes with garlic and oil.

5.   Transfer to the grill plate and close the hood.

6.   In a separate bowl, mix the vinegar, olive oil, lime juice, pepper flakes, salt, dill, pepper, green onions, and cinnamon. Whisk.

7.   Transfer the grilled bacon and potatoes to a bowl and drizzle with the vinegar dressing.

Serving suggestions: Serve immediately

Preparation and Cooking Tips: Flip the items on the grill plate halfway

Nutritional value per serving: Calories: 170kcal, Fat: 3g, Carb: 5g, Proteins: 12g

Chapter 15: Roasting Recipes

Roasted Pumpkin

This meal results in a delightful recipe that can be served for different types of occasion

Preparation time: 10 minutes
Cooking time: 12 minutes
Serves: 4

Ingredients To Use:
- sea salt, a pinch
- 1½ pound of pumpkin, pitted and chopped
- cinnamon powder, a pinch
- 3 garlic cloves, grated
- brown sugar, a pinch
- 1 Tbsp of olive oil
- ground nutmeg, a pinch

Step-by-Step Directions to Cook It:
1. Place the cooking pot and crisper basket into the Ninja Foodi Grill and ensure the splatter shield is positioned. Close the hood.
2. Press the Roast button. Set the temperature to 370°F and adjust the time to 12 minutes.
3. Press the start/stop button to preheat the appliance for 3 minutes.
4. Mix the pumpkin, salt, sugar, oil, cinnamon, nutmeg, and garlic in a bowl.
5. Transfer to the crisper basket and close the hood

Serving suggestions: Serve as a side dish

Preparation and Cooking Tips: Shake the basket halfway

Nutritional value per serving: Calories: 200kcal, Fat: 5g, Carb: 7g, Proteins: 4g

Parmesan Mushrooms

Try this recipe now and watch how fast you demand a second helping

Preparation time: 10 minutes
Cooking time: 20 minutes
Serves: 6

Ingredients To Use:
- 2 Tbsp of chopped parsley
- 5 garlic cloves, grated
- ½ tsp of dried basil
- ½ tsp of dried oregano
- 3 pounds of halved red potatoes
- 1 tsp of dried thyme
- 2 Tbsp of olive oil
- Salt and black pepper, as desired
- 2 Tbsp of butter
- 1/3 cup of grated parmesan

Step-by-Step Directions to Cook It:
1. Place the cooking pot into the Ninja Foodi Grill and ensure the splatter shield is in position. Close the hood.
2. Press the Roast button. Set the temperature to 400°F and adjust the time to 20 minutes.
3. Press the start/stop button to preheat the appliance for 3 minutes.
4. Mix the potato halves, garlic, parsley, oregano, basil, thyme, pepper, salt, butter, and oil in a bowl.

5.   Transfer the coated potatoes to the cooking pot and close the hood.

Serving suggestions: Top with parmesan and serve as a side dish

Preparation and Cooking Tips: Flip the potatoes halfway

Nutritional value per serving: Calories: 162kcal, Fat: 5g, Carb: 7g, Proteins: 5g

Foodi Roasted Carrots

Roasted carrots have a crunchy and delicious taste that keeps you asking for more

Preparation time: 10 minutes
Cooking time: 20 minutes
Serves: 4

Ingredients To Use:
- 4 Tbsp of orange juice
- 1 pound of baby carrots
- 1 tsp of herbs de Provence
- 2 tsp of olive oil

Step-by-Step Directions to Cook It:
1.   Place the cooking pot and crisper basket into the Ninja Foodi Grill and ensure the splatter shield is in position. Close the hood.
2.   Press the Roast button. Set the temperature to 320°F and adjust the time to 20 minutes.
3.   Press the start/stop button to preheat the appliance for 3 minutes.
4.   Season the carrots with the herbs de Provence, orange juice, and oil.
5.   Transfer to the crisper basket and close the hood.

Serving suggestions: Serve as a side dish

Preparation and Cooking Tips: Shake the basket halfway

Nutritional value per serving: Calories: 112kcal, Fat: 2g, Carb: 4g, Proteins: 3g

Vermouth Mushrooms

Vermouth mushroom has got a unique taste. It is delicious and will keep you craving for more.

Preparation time: 10 minutes
Cooking time: 25 minutes
Serves: 4

Ingredients To Use:
- 2 garlic cloves, grated
- 1 Tbsp of olive oil
- 2 pounds of white mushrooms
- 2 tsp of herbs de Provence
- 2 Tbsp of white vermouth

Step-by-Step Directions to Cook It:
1.   Place the cooking pot into the Ninja Foodi Grill and ensure the splatter shield is in position. Close the hood.
2.   Press the Roast button. Set the temperature to 350°F and adjust the time to 20 minutes.
3.   Press the start/stop button to preheat the appliance for 3 minutes.
4.   Combine the herbs de Provence, mushrooms, garlic, and oil.
5.   Transfer to the cooking pot and close the hood.
6.   Add the vermouth and increase the timer by 5 minutes.

Serving suggestions: Serve as a side dish

Preparation and Cooking Tips: Flip food regularly

Nutritional value per serving: Calories: 121kcal, Fat: 2g, Carb: 7g, Proteins: 4g

Roasted Parsnips

Roasted parsnips have got a crunchy taste that sets them apart from regular parsnip meals.
Preparation time: 10 minutes
Cooking time: 40 minutes
Serves: 6
Ingredients To Use:
• 2 pounds of parsnips, chopped into medium chunks
• 2 Tbsp of maple syrup
• 1 Tbsp of dried parsley flakes
• 1 Tbsp of olive oil
Step-by-Step Directions to Cook It:
1. Place the cooking pot into the Ninja Foodi Grill and ensure the splatter shield is in position. Close the hood.
2. Press the Roast button. Set the temperature to 360°F and adjust the time to 45 minutes.
3. Press the start/stop button to preheat the appliance for 3 minutes.
4. Coat the parsnip with oil, parsley flakes, and maple syrup.
5. Transfer to the cooking pot and close the hood.
  Serving suggestions: Serve as a side dish
Preparation and Cooking Tips: Flip the parsnip halfway
Nutritional value per serving: Calories: 124kcal, Fat: 3g, Carb: 7g, Proteins: 4g

Ninja Glazed Beets

Glazed beets are delicious and nutritious. It can be enjoyed as dinner or lunch.
Preparation time: 10 minutes
Cooking time: 40 minutes
Serves: 8
Ingredients To Use:
• 3 pounds of trimmed small beets
• 4 Tbsp of maple syrup
• 1 Tbsp of melted duck fat
Step-by-Step Directions to Cook It:
1. Place the cooking pot into the Ninja Foodi Grill and ensure the splatter shield is in position. Close the hood.
2. Press the Roast button. Set the temperature to 360°F and adjust the time to 4o minutes.
3. Press the start/stop button to preheat the appliance for 3 minutes.
4. Coat the beets with the duck fat and male syrup.
5. Transfer the coated beets to the cooking pot and close the hood.
  Serving suggestions: Serve immediately
Preparation and Cooking Tips: Flip the beets halfway
Nutritional value per serving: Calories: 121kcal, Fat: 3g, Carb: 3g, Proteins: 4g

Carrots and Rhubarb

Carrots and rhubarb are awesome. They taste great and require minimal preparation.
Preparation time: 10 minutes
Cooking time: 40 minutes

Serves: 4
Ingredients To Use:
- ½ tsp of stevia
- 1 pound of baby carrots
- 1 pound of roughly chopped rhubarb
- 1 orange, cut into medium segments and zest grated
- 2 tsp of walnut oil
- ½ cup halved walnuts

Step-by-Step Directions to Cook It:
1. Place the cooking pot into the Ninja Foodi Grill and ensure the splatter shield is in position. Close the hood.
2. Press the Roast button. Set the temperature to 380°F and adjust the time to 20 minutes.
3. Press the start/stop button to preheat the appliance for 3 minutes.
4. In a bowl, combine the carrots and oil.
5. Add the rhubarbs, stevia, orange zest, and walnuts.
6. Transfer the mixture to the cooking pot and close the hood.

Serving suggestions: Top with orange segments and serve
Preparation and Cooking Tips: Flip the food halfway
Nutritional value per serving: Calories: 172kcal, Fat: 2g, Carb: 4g, Proteins: 4g

Ninja Roasted Eggplants

Roasted eggplants are crunchy, tasty, and perfect for weight loss. Try this recipe out now
Preparation time: 10 minutes
Cooking time: 20 minutes

Serves: 6
Ingredients To Use:
- ½ lemon, juiced
- 1½ pounds of cubed eggplants
- 2 bay leaves
- 2 tsp of za'atar
- 1 Tbsp of olive oil
- 1 tsp of onion powder
- 1 tsp of sumac
- 1 tsp of garlic powder

Step-by-Step Directions to Cook It:
1. Place the cooking pot into the Ninja Foodi Grill and ensure the splatter shield is in position. Close the hood.
2. Press the Roast button. Set the temperature to 370°F and adjust the time to 20 minutes.
3. Press the start/stop button to preheat the appliance for 3 minutes.
4. Mix the onion powder, garlic powder, za'atar, lemon juice, sumac, bay leaves, and oil in a bowl
5. Add the eggplants and stir until well coated.

Serving suggestions: Serve as a side dish
Preparation and Cooking Tips: Flip the eggplants halfway
Nutritional value per serving: Calories: 172kcal, Fat: 4g, Carb: 12g, Proteins: 3g

Roasted Potato Chips

Potato chips are usually not healthy, but with the minimal oil requirement of the Ninja Foodi grill, this meal is diet-friendly.
Preparation time: 30 minutes
Cooking time: 30 minutes

Serves: 4

Ingredients To Use:
- 1 Tbsp of olive oil
- 4 potatoes, peeled and cut into thin chips, rinsed, soaked for 30 minutes, drained and dried with paper towels
- Salt, as desired
- 2 tsp of chopped rosemary

Step-by-Step Directions to Cook It:
1. Place the cooking pot and crisper basket into the Ninja Foodi Grill and ensure the splatter shield is in position. Close the hood.
2. Press the Roast button. Set the temperature to 330°F and adjust the time to 30 minutes.
3. Press the start/stop button to preheat the appliance for 3 minutes.
4. Mix the potato chips, oil, and salt in a bowl. Toss until well coated.
5. Transfer to the crisper basket and close the hood

Serving suggestions: Top with rosemary

Preparation and Cooking Tips: Shake the crisper basket halfway

Nutritional value per serving: Calories: 200kcal, Fat: 4g, Carb: 14g, Proteins: 5g

Roasted Tortillas

Tortillas taste great, especially when prepared with the Ninja Foodi Grill

Preparation time: 10 minutes
Cooking time: 6 minutes
Serves: 4

Ingredients To Use:
- sweet paprika, a pinch
- 8 corn tortillas, divided into shapes
- garlic powder, a pinch
- 1 Tbsp of olive oil
- Salt and black pepper, as desired

Step-by-Step Directions to Cook It:
1. Place the cooking pot and crisper basket into the Ninja Foodi Grill and ensure the splatter shield is positioned. Close the hood.
2. Press the Roast button. Set the temperature to 400°F and adjust the time to 6 minutes.
3. Press the start/stop button to preheat the appliance for 3 minutes.
4. Mix the tortilla chips, salt, pepper, paprika, garlic powder, and oil in a bowl.
5. Transfer the seasoned chips to the crisper basket and close the hood.

Serving suggestions: Serve as a side dish

Preparation and Cooking Tips: Shake the crisper basket halfway

Nutritional value per serving: Calories: 53kcal, Fat: 1g, Carb: 6g, Proteins: 4g

Conclusion

With any of the Ninja Foodi Grills, you need only a few ingredients, some essential spices, and a good recipe book from yours truly :) to make as many delicious meals as you like.

Good luck!

Printed in the USA
CPSIA information can be obtained
at www.ICGtesting.com
LVHW012122041123
762867LV00006B/52